PENGUIN BOOKS

AN ABSOLUTELY OUTRAGEOUS ADVENTURE

JOHN BOUGEN is a successful Auckland property
developer and a passionate traveller.

JILL MALCOLM is an award-winning travel writer.

It is our duty to proceed from what is near to what is distant, to what is now to that which is less known. To gather the traditions from those who have reported them, to correct them as much as possible and leave the rest as it is, in order to make our work help anyone who seeks truth and loves wisdom.

Abdu'l Rayhan Mohammet-i-Burini (973 –1050)

an ABSOLUTELY OUTRAGEOUS ADVENTURE

John Bougen

and

Jill Malcolm

PENGUIN BOOKS

To crazy bastards everywhere

PENGUIN BOOKS
Published by the Penguin Group
Penguin Books (NZ) Ltd, cnr Airborne and Rosedale Roads, Albany,
Auckland 1310, New Zealand
Penguin Books Ltd, 80 Strand, London, WC2R 0RL, England
Penguin Group (USA) Inc., 375 Hudson Street, New York, NY 10014, United States
Penguin Books Australia Ltd, 250 Camberwell Road, Camberwell,
Victoria 3124, Australia
Penguin Books Canada Ltd, 10 Alcorn Avenue, Toronto,
Ontario, Canada M4V 3B2
Penguin Books (South Africa) (Pty) Ltd, 24 Sturdee Avenue, Rosebank,
Johannesburg 2196, South Africa
Penguin Books India (P) Ltd, 11, Community Centre, Panchsheel Park,
New Delhi 110 017, India
Penguin Books Ltd, Registered Offices: 80 Strand, London, WC2R 0RL, England

First published by Penguin Books (NZ) Ltd, 2003
1 3 5 7 9 10 8 6 4 2
Copyright © John Bougen
Copyright © photographs John Bougen

The right of Jill Malcolm to be identified as the author of this work in terms of
section 96 of the Copyright Act 1994 is hereby asserted.

Designed by Mary Egan
Typeset by Egan-Reid Ltd
Printed in Australia by McPherson's Printing Group

ISBN 0 14 301880 9
A catalogue record for this book is available
from the National Library of New Zealand.

www.penguin.co.nz

contents

ACKNOWLEDGEMENTS

The inspiration for the All Nations Quest, and consequently this book, remains nameless: he is the Deputy Headmaster of a secondary school in the central North Island of New Zealand, who one Monday morning said on National Radio that he was to receive a silver medal from an International Travel Club for visiting 150 countries. I look forward to shaking his hand one day and extending a very big thank you for instilling in me an idea that came to consume my every waking moment.

However, our wives and family may not necessarily share this view. Anna, my long-suffering wife of twenty years, and our daughter, Nic, then aged eighteen and preoccupied with her own adventures, along with James' wife Nicola, were forced to share yet another of my hair-brained schemes. Few of my cunning ideas see the light of day, but this time, after nine months of intensive, all-consuming planning and dreaming, we boarded our first flight on 28 August 2002, much to the bewilderment of us all.

Anna, Nic and Nicola bore the brunt of our total absorption in a ludicrous venture, both pre- and post-Quest, and to them we proffer our love, gratitude and, somewhat belatedly, our apologies for not always being there for them while we were occupied with the imponderables of travelling the world.

Thanks to a host of individuals, both friends and business associates, who in the ultimate show of love and friendship did what we should have been doing, but couldn't on account of distance, time zones and being completely distracted with the matter at hand. My father-in-law, Graeme Edwards, went one better by extending words of wisdom and the balm of logic to placate those both away and at home.

Many questioned our sanity. Happily, some came forward with impressive knowledge, product and much-needed sponsorship that made our dream come true: Chris Grieve, Ann Torsonsen and the entire team at Flight Centre; nzoom's Glyn Jones and Sidah Russell; Chris Dobbs from Working Style; Geoff Johnson from Brandex; the last minute but no less appreciated Vodafone marketers, Jill Donnachie and Lynley Kirk-Smith; Mike Henry of the travel insurance company that bears his name; Pedro from Translation Fast; Dean McLachlan, Jill Beasley and Jody Gill of Publicis Drum; Fiona Newton and Georgie Clatworthy who kept the wheels turning, along with Paul Blomfield and Leanne Hayden.

The unstinting efforts of Vaughan Ludlam who thought he was to join a property development company and spent the first nine months organising visas, train schedules, road condition reports and the production of the three record books remains integral to our success.

None of the journey would have been recorded had not Jill Malcolm, after three months of pestering, agreed to write the book. If I had known how much work was involved in getting this missive to print then quite possibly the concept would have been snuffed out at its inception. It was only Jill's persistence, enthusiasm and humour that turned our musings into print.

Why it did get finished is due to the almost divine guidance from the good folks at Penguin Books: Bernice Beachman and Philippa Gerrard kept us honest, enthused and toiling, confident always that we would complete what we had ambitiously said we would do.

Much of what is told herein is only possible because of the uncomplaining assistance from a horde of individuals around the world. Kiwis are everywhere, as we can truly now testify. Our gratitude goes to Paula Duffy for making the impossible happen in Djibouti and Somalia; Stephen, Therese and Christopher for calming us in Switzerland; Kim and Todd Forrester in Singapore; Andy Cole, his wife Lara Fosi and their neighbours Tina and Dave in Ouagadougou; Mathew Towse at Almaty airport; Peter, Geli, Oliver and Alissa Fulton who made Dubai a Christmas home away from home, and Kevin Kluts who came to our accommodation rescue in Ottawa.

Others are probably still unaware of how much their assistance meant to us. We remain indebted to Paul from Radio LMFM, Ireland; Balde who continues to survive Conakry, Guinea; Kledi Milloshi, aka Clint, whom we met at the Macedonian/Albanian border; Dr Monica Nolan for speaking English and sense; Rolando and Bianca Altagracia for waiting in vain; Ammar Mohamed from the Protocol Department at Baghdad Airport (we trust you followed your ex-leader's example and survived the US invasion); Osvaldo Gomes for supporting material; Utz Wellner for his views on just about everything Pacific; Ambassador Mamatsashvili and consul Konstantin Surguladze for making the acquisition of a Georgian visa an experience worth repeating; Rashed Ahmed Ali Al-Noaimi and Ahmed Salah of Bahrain's Border Immigration service for getting us to where no Saudi Arabian wanted us to go – in particular Saudi Arabia; Scott Walter for always being at the end of an Internet signal and making spreadsheet sense of our travels; Peter and Sally Jackson for never saying why; Ants Jackson for giving us a logo to fly beneath; Alice and all of the Templetons along with Ben and the Dowdles, Samantha and the Bowers, Robyn and the Bougens and Stuart Irving for keeping us grounded and in touch with home.

One Kiwi that went everywhere with us was Phil Goff, New Zealand's Minister of Foreign Affairs and Trade. Phil, your letter and photo saved our bacon on countless occasions. To this day, there are a number of immigration officials who are somewhat bemused that a minister of foreign affairs would be travelling with an entourage of one (namely James) and in economy class. It appears to some that we have a similarity of facial features.

Special thanks to Save the Children for giving us the reason to travel, and assistance and insights that will haunt and inspire us for years. Liz Gibbs, Rachel Fahey and John Bovis of Save the Children New Zealand; Philip Crabtree from Oslo, Norway; Carolyn Miles and Karen Quigley of the Westport USA Head Office; the Los Angeles team of Faye Docuyanan and Leandra Woods, and the dedicated team of Sally Griffin, Tim Barker, Albertina Muchanga and Etelvina da Cunha who continue to battle against HIV/Aids and just about everything else in Quelimane, Mozambique.

Finally, and while it sounds a bit naff it is said with heart-felt meaning, we owe eternal gratitude to our late mothers, sisters Doreen and Jean, for passing on a love of travel and crossing new borders.

ACKNOWLEDGEMENTS

30 June 2003

Hon Phil Goff
Minister of Foreign Affairs and Trade
Parliament Buildings
Wellington
New Zealand

Dear Phil

Some 10 months ago, you kindly gave up a good portion of your Saturday morning to sign a letter of support that we had had translated into six different languages and then bound into three separate 'All Nations Quest Record Books'.

Thanks in large part to your letter and photo we were able to set a number of world records, including the most nations visited in a single journey – 191 in 167 days. As you rightly pointed out in your letter 'This record attempt will test their endurance to the limit' and it did. As our wives will attest, it took a few months for the adrenalin levels to abate to a level where 'normal' life could be tackled with a degree of enthusiasm. Given your current travel schedule, you will have a complete understanding of the effect that 167 days of Nation bashing has on the system.

Quite frankly had we not had your translated letter, then it is unlikely that we would have been able to enter, or for that matter exit, ten or so countries. To this day there are immigration officials in Chad, D.R. Congo, and Tajikistan who are still perplexed as to why a Minister of Foreign Affairs would be travelling with a support party of one and in economy class. It appears that to some we have similar facial features.

Two books relating to the Quest have been commissioned by Penguin. The first to be entitled 'An Absolutely Outrageous Adventure' will be released in September 2003 and the second 'My Dream', which records the pictures and dreams of 100 or so children from 100 different countries, will be released in October 2003. Part of the sale proceeds from 'My Dream' will be going to the Save the Children Fund, being a continuation of the profile raising that we accomplished for them, both at home and on our travels.

We only missed out on two nations – Sao Tome and Principe and Afghanistan. Both as it transpired through totally full flights and a shortage of time on our part to hang around until seats became available.

The next trick is to knock off the Territories of the world, which over the next year or two will be the next Quest. If you happen to have a free seat on a Hercules going to say the Antarctica, then I would be happy to help you out by filling it.

Thankyou again for your assistance. It allowed us to achieve our dream. We remain indebted.

Sincerely

John Bougen
All Nations Quest
www.allnationsquest.com

Hon Phil Goff,
Minister of Foreign Affairs and Trade,
August 2002

Goff wishes kiwi duo well on record-breaking travel attempt

New Zealanders have a love of travel which is perhaps borne out of our geographical isolation and a thirst to see the rest of the world. But there is also a natural kiwi sense of adventure to explore and experience the planet.

It is that spirit which encapsulates this audacious bid by John Bougen and James Irving to travel to 193 countries in less than 160 days.

But this is not all about breaking records. John and James pledge to use their travels to raise the profile of the Save The Children charity is an important and admirable goal.

As a Foreign Minister I know how punishing a busy travel schedule can be. Crossing datelines and encountering a myriad of cultures and customs while fascinating and fulfilling can also be exhausting. This record attempt will test their endurance to the limit.

I wish John and James all the best on their travels and support for their attempt to raise the profile of such a worthy charity.

PHIL GOFF
MINISTER OF FOREIGN AFFAIRS

The world is a book, and those who do not travel read only a page.

Augustine (354–430)

CHAPTER ONE

Take-off

It was a crazy idea. That's the reason the thought wouldn't go away. For some people crazy ideas have a fascination that present as a challenge. And I'd always found a challenge irresistible.

This one came bolting out of the blue when my career had hit a bit of a hiatus. All the businesses I was involved in had CEOs who were coping perfectly well without me and I couldn't see any immediate challenges ahead. Then cruising down the motorway one Saturday morning, with half an ear tuned to the radio, I heard a deputy headmaster from a school in the central North Island talking about how he was off to somewhere in the world to receive a medal from an international travel club because he'd been to 150 countries. Inwardly, I scoffed. I'd been to a hell of a lot more countries than that.

The next day I was flying out to Los Angeles on business and spent the whole trip thumbing through my passport working out just how many places I had been to. I was shocked to find that I'd even been travel-trumped by my wife. I'd been overseas 128 times in the last nine years but only to 28 different countries. I'm a pretty competitive person and quite frankly I was gutted.

For the next few months I couldn't leave it alone. I spent hours trying to work out, hypothetically, how I could get someone to fund me not only to beat that man's record but also, as an even whackier idea, to go to every country in the world. I came to the early conclusion that if I wanted to do it, I'd have to pay for it myself.

'Madness, madness. Can't be done,' said friends and family. Had they forgotten that doing things that other people say can't be done has always been my greatest motivation?

On the wall in my study hangs a framed draughtsman's sketch of a letterbox, a memento of my first foray into the world of new ideas. When I was 14, I went into the letterbox business with a mate of mine, Dub Steel. I asked my father's architect friend to come up with a design; Dub and I saved our pocket money; bought a huge amount of timber; cut it all up; painted it — and then ran out of steam. Dub's parents wanted their garage back and I ended up taking most of the timber home. Mum burned it in the fire for the next 10 years.

It was a fiery end to a good thought, but it taught me not to be scared of setting my ideas alight. Taking a chance, even if you miss out, has always been more exciting for me than guaranteed success.

There has been a string of new enterprises and businesses since. The latest was the Auckland Memorial Park cemetery my partners and I developed at Silverdale, with excellent feng shui and a heavenly host of imaginative packages for the dead and about to be buried. The idea for the cemetery came to me when my father had died and none of the existing burial places provided the breadth of choice that I would have liked. There were just too many restrictions.

But it was at my mother's funeral two years later that another event put the every-country-in-the-world idea within reach. I re-met my cousin James Irving. He'd been born in New Zealand but shifted to Australia 15 years ago and we'd had little to do with each other. I discovered he lived in Brisbane. My wife Anna and I often go to the Gold Coast, and I suggested that he and his wife Nicola get together with us for a meal. Over the next four years I suppose we met about five times.

And then sitting with him on the balcony of his home on a balmy Queensland evening around Christmas 2001 with the light of the city vying with the stars and fruit bats flitting around the trees, the conversation turned to the ultimate trip. Would it be possible to go to every country in the world in the space of about three months? James has been a travel agent all his life and he took up the hypothetical challenge immediately. I remember we both got pretty excited. In the end I said to James in a musing sort of way, 'We should just do it.'

'Well, okay, yes,' he said.

Neither of us had any conviction at that point that these things would come to pass, but that night was when we decided to go through the exercise.

James had been successful in his career, part-owning at one point his own specialist travel agency in Sydney. He was now a senior member of a large travel company in Brisbane but he was feeling restless and he relished the thought of getting his teeth into something new. The first task was to find out how many countries there actually were. I bought a *Guinness Book of Records* and discovered that the most-travelled people in the world were Dr Robert Becker and his wife Carmen of Pompano Beach, Florida, who had met during World War II and since then had travelled to 234 countries. We would have to visit 235 to make sure we beat their record.

I wrote to the Guinness people who suggested that instead we set a record for going to every nation in the world in a single journey using scheduled services. For that purpose the term 'nation' included the 189 countries that belonged to the United Nations plus East Timor, Taiwan, Vatican City and Switzerland. Our adventure became known as the All Nations Quest.

James started working on the itinerary and visas, which meant contacting countries he'd never heard of, let alone airlines – a mind-blowing task. He worked with the Flight Centre but soon learned that even with their combined experience it wasn't going to be easy. We would need to make about 250 flights, which would take around five months.

We'd get one schedule done and then one sector would fall over and he would have to go back and do the whole thing again. That happened three or four times. With Africa, for instance, many airlines hadn't confirmed their schedules for the year ahead. Some only have incoming flights once or twice a week; others didn't talk to their neighbours. We decided to buy a 35 sector around-the-world-ticket for a start – business-class so it could be flexible – and then build economy-class side itineraries into it. One delayed or missed flight could dramatically affect the rest of the itinerary so we also built in a few time-buffers. The ticket portfolio we ended up with was enormous – 30 different tickets, many with up to 10 sectors. When opened out they reached over six metres in length.

Meanwhile, I was dashing about with unquenchable optimism, sorting the itinerary, visas, sponsorships, vaccinations, publicity and my less-than-enthusiastic family.

Forty visas were needed before we left. One passport each was not going to do it and special dispensation had to be given so that we could each hold three.

Vaughan Ludlam, who worked for me, became expert at the meticulous juggling of passports around the world. Most visas were valid until three months after the date of issue so we had to ensure they didn't expire before they were needed. My office at home was festooned with ever-changing schedules, timetables and maps. I had three logbooks printed with forewords by the

Minister of Foreign Affairs, Phil Goff, and then translated into six languages. To satisfy the requirement of the *Guinness Book of Records* we needed the signature of a witness in every nation. We endured 17 vaccinations, bought multiple backpacks until I found the perfect one, organised public relations and media contacts, bought a state-of-the-art videocam, a digital camera, laptop and cellphones, and tried to drum up sponsorship.

The sponsorship support was disappointing. Flight Centre was very enthusiastic, and so was nzoom, the digital magazine of Television New Zealand, which undertook to run a website containing reports of the journey which I would send them from the road. But there was little else.

In the absence of support for ourselves, we decided to try and find an official charity that might benefit from the journey. Save the Children Fund was keen to come on board, offering practical assistance, if needed, in the countries where they operated. In return we would ask for donations to the cause through our website. But the best idea was to develop another book. I would use my skills as a photographer to take a picture of a child in every country and ask that child, 'If any one of your dreams could come true – what would it be?' This gave the trip the purpose it had previously lacked.

A few days before departure, when he had flown over from Australia, James was expending a lot of effort trying not to look tense, which gave him the appearance of a small boy being forced to stand still. At times he talked too much to relieve his anxiety. 'You know, at first I didn't take this idea too seriously,' he said. 'Over the next few months I thought, "Well, if it never happens it's still been worth the ride because in terms of my knowledge it's been a monumental exercise and I've enjoyed it." I'd left my job, finalised arrangements for my absence, but it wasn't really until I packed on the last night at home that I acknowledged that this was no longer a pipe dream.'

The day before the departure there was a flurry of media interest and come-lately sponsors. Vodafone suddenly wanted to be involved and came up with a package of free phone time and state-of-the-art cellphone accessories. Brandex sent two pairs of Jetskins — full-length stockings to ward off deep-vein thrombosis — and Mike Henry Insurance came through with a comprehensive insurance policy.

On 28 August 2002, late in the afternoon, we met at the airport. Only a handful of people had gathered to wave goodbye: Anna, my wife, our 18-year-old daughter Nic, Anna's father Graeme, my sister Diana and family; Vaughan and Dean; Glyn and Sidah from nzoom, Jill Malcolm who was to write the book about the journey and a television cameraman crew who ordered up a few mock farewells and waves.

As people do at departure time, we stood around in a strained little group making flippant comments about the weather and the time and how the Warriors league team had lost so resoundingly to the Newcastle Knights the night before, as jolly as if we were merely departing for a trip to Christchurch for the weekend.

We went to check in. I returned indignant that the Qantas attendant had merely glanced at my bulging ticket and droned, 'Off on a bit of a trip, are you, sir?'

Anna and Nic were relieved the time had finally come. When it was time, the goodbyes were brief: a few good lucks, a few last-minute instructions and cheek pecks. Then the friends and relatives melted away. Dressed in our crisp new khaki shirts embroidered with sponsors' logos, carrying small backpacks loaded with everything we would need for the next five months, we wandered into the departing crowd as if we were strolling along St Heliers Beach on a Sunday afternoon.

It felt marvellous stowing the baggage in the overhead locker, sinking into the comfortable blue business-class seats of the Lan Chile aircraft, the reality still hovering around waiting for me to grasp it.

All the last-minute things – around the house, the paperwork, organising, packing and re-packing, the panic, the family reactions, the things that didn't happen that irritated me and the things I didn't want to happen that did – receded the minute I hit the seat.

James and I both felt elated. We toasted our success thus far with a glass of champagne.

This first flight and, at 9647 kilometres the longest of the journey, passed in luxury. We needed the rest, the comfort and attention we felt we deserved. We basked in its reassurance, aware that such ease wouldn't last for the next five months.

23 BAHAMAS

24 JAMAICA

22 HAITI 21 DOMINICAN REPUBLIC

20 ST KITTS & NEVIS
18 ANTIGUA & BARBUDA
19 DOMINICA
17 ST LUCIA
15 ST VINCENT & THE GRENADINES
16 BARBADOS
14 GRENADA

CARIBBEAN SEA

11 TRINIDAD & TOBAGO

10 VENEZUELA

13 GUYANA

9 COLOMBIA

12 SURINAME

8 ECUADOR

7 PERU

4 BRAZIL

6 BOLIVIA

5 PARAGUAY

1 CHILE

3 URUGUAY

2 ARGENTINA

CHAPTER TWO

SOUTH America, SOUTH

1 Chile

Eleven hours later, at five minutes past midday on the same day we had left New Zealand, we landed in Santiago. A heavy smog hung about the airport lending a surreal quality to our arrival. Outside the terminal we were mobbed by rogue (non-registered) taxi drivers and negotiated the 45-minute ride to downtown Santiago.

Our pressing need was to organise a visa for Paraguay, which we hadn't managed to do from New Zealand. The Paraguayan Consulate was on the fifth floor of a humble building with a waiting room so small it could accommodate only three people at a time. The carpet was threadbare, the walls shabby and unadorned. Behind a glazed hole in the wall sat the Consul General of Paraguay, a small-boned swarthy fellow with a heavy moustache who was paying business-like attention to the matter in hand. We filled in forms and were fingerprinted.

'Your visas will be with you in less than a day,' he assured us. We were stunned by such efficiency.

James was determined we should walk back to the hotel as a start for his exercise regime. 'Half an hour's walk and I've earned a beer,' he said. He'd been urged to try Quilmes Crystal, which apparently would cure jetlag. It didn't.

A short walk turned out to be four hours. We first stopped for an espresso at the Café Caribe where the startling Latin beauty of the waitresses and the length, or rather the lack of it, of their skirts probably accounted for the large male patronage. Then we came upon the Museum of Natural History which intrigued us for an hour despite explanations being only in Spanish; and when we finally struck out for the hotel, James' solar and gut-feel method of navigation turned out to be decidedly vague.

The people we saw in downtown Santiago were well-groomed, darkly attractive and stylish in fashionably tailored leather coats. This was not true of all Santiago. Next day we drove past large areas of very poor slums and a rubbish tip where there were hovels in among the piles of garbage. Here there was no style at all.

A funicular railway climbs up to the summit of San Cristobel mountain from where there are, by all accounts, stunning views of the city and the surrounding mountains. Later in the day we took the ride but the enveloping swirls of 'fug' ensured that we saw nothing.

In the morning we went to the New Zealand Embassy to have the logbook signed for the first time, and took our first photograph for the children's book. Three small children were leaning against a stone wall with their mothers close by. We used sign language, pointing to the camera and holding the book out to indicate what we wanted.

Paloma, Geria and Catalina lived on the streets. Catalina was a beautiful raven-haired little girl of about three and she loved being photographed, posing with her big brown eyes firmly fixed on the camera lens, glancing occasionally at her mother for approval and then throwing a coquettish grin in our direction. I asked her, through a bystander who interpreted, what her dream for the future was.

'Tener una casa,' she said. 'I want a house.'

2 Argentina

A day later, the flight on Lan Chile to Buenos Aires crossed the Andes in just over 10 minutes. We marvelled at their jagged, snow-spangled peaks and enormous scale. On the Argentinian side the land flattened into the vast, fertile pampas grasslands where the gaucho cattle herders had established the country's huge beef industry. There was little sign of habitation until 30 minutes out from the city when lakes and small towns started appearing.

Argentina's economic situation was dismal. Inflation was around 30 percent a year and a quarter of the population was unemployed. When we had booked the Ibis Hotel nine months ago the price had been $US200 per night. It was now $US25, which indicated what had happened to the peso in the meantime.

Through our website we'd been communicating with Rob Mumford, a New Zealander who lived in Buenos Aires. He'd warned of a demonstration that was planned for the night we arrived. 'Today is a day of protests and demonstrations,' he wrote. 'Downtown there'll be a huge march from Congress to the Plaza de Mayo. It could get violent. People are sick of poverty, unemployment and government corruption.'

When we arrived at the hotel, a large crowd was already forming in the adjacent Plaza Congresso. There were small

Rob Mumford
and Natalia,
Buenos Aires.

children and grandparents as well as feisty young men and women. When the march began it was peaceful but exceedingly clamorous. Singers screamed their protest into microphones, marchers chorused their slogans, drummers whipped up the tempo and firecrackers exploded like gunfire.

It could hardly be ignored and, against advice, James and I joined in. I was focussed on taking photographs and was swept away in a current of humanity. I lost James and when I next saw him he was striding along beside a row of drummers, still dressed in his rolled-up shirtsleeves, so absorbed by all the activity that he hadn't noticed how cold it was.

This march was the most vibrant, impassioned, high-energy event I had ever seen. I was mesmerised by two young female singers with great voices who stood on the back of a truck belting out a protest song so hauntingly intense that it dragged me along in its wake.

After an hour we extricated ourselves and headed south down Avenue 9 de Julio, the city's widest boulevard. It was almost deserted except for small huddles of federal police who were diplomatically positioned one block away from the protesters so as to provide as little provocation as possible – a crowd of protesters hyped to the max could easily have turned ugly.

The mob receded into the distance and the contrasting silence in the boulevard was eerie. We felt as if we had scuttled like cowards from the scene of battle. We took the opportunity to have the record book witnessed (as the *Guinness Book of Records* required) by a person of authority, the burly Officer 307, who wore a thick Kevlar bulletproof vest. He insisted that James also sit on his four-wheel ATV motorbike to have his photograph taken.

We made our way to Puerto Madero, a former docklands now converted to accommodate a row of about 30 modern restaurants, and enjoyed an excellent meal of beef and salads and a very fine Argentinian cabernet sauvignon for an affordable $NZ60 for two. But I got the exchange rate wrong, and the waiter could just about have bought the restaurant with what I tipped him. No wonder he ushered us to the door. Back at the hotel we fell into comfortable beds and slept for 10 hours, which banished most of the lingering daze of jetlag.

We were having trouble with communications. There was no mobile phone signal, no Internet access and landline connections were out. We later discovered the reason – thieves were stealing the phone wire. Since January, 5000 kilometres of copper wire had been removed from the national telephone system, causing massive disruption. Copper had quadrupled in value since the start of 2002 and could be sold for foreign currency. The government increased the export duty on copper scrap fivefold, but it was too late for the country's beleaguered communication system. We made up our own protest slogan: 'Don't try for me in Argentina.'

The next day we met Rob Mumford and his daughter Natalia outside the main gates of the Recoletta Cemetaria. We were still on Chilean time and had kept them waiting patiently for us in the bitterly cold piazza for an hour. Rob, a 37-year-old Wellingtonian, had lived in Argentina for the last four years. 'I came here in 1990 as a backpacker,' he told us, 'and fell in love with the place – the dramatic landscapes, the passionate people and, in particular, a beautiful local girl called Laura.' Natalia is their daughter, a vivacious nine-year-old with her mother's deep Latin eyes and a cascade of curly black hair.

'The country's problems are huge,' he said, 'but it's a place with a strong spirit.' He guided us around the cemetery where many famous Argentinians are buried, including Eva Peron who is interred in a huge dark marble mausoleum hung with brass plaques placed there by her admirers. There was just time to share a large plate of empanadas at Café Americano with Rob and Natalia before we bid them *adios* and headed for the Jorge Newbury Airoporto.

On the way I practised some newly acquired Spanish on the taxi driver.

'*Español bien*?' I finished.

'Mister, you punish *Español*,' he said in heavily accented English.

The final approach to the runway for incoming aircraft is directly above the riverside autopiste (motorway) that leads into the departure terminal. Hearing a vintage Aerolineas Argentinas Boeing 737 about 10 metres above us and then seeing it slew dangerously to port, with one wing nearly touching the ground, had us both making futile ducking motions. Our driver didn't turn a hair.

The *aeroporto* was magnificently sited on the banks of the Rio de la Plata and through the wide windows of the terminal the river and city spread to the horizon. We checked in for the onward journey to Montevideo and waited with the rest of the passengers for security to amble to their stations. We would have to get used to South American timings.

3 Uruguay

We landed in this small country, which is northeast of Argentina and bordered to the south by the estuary of the Rio de la Plata, at terrifying speed. Whiling away the time in the immigration queue, it was hard not to notice a 2-metre high sign which read: 'Sanitary Barrier. Stop. It is forbidden to enter any animal or vegetel product.' I wondered if there was a Society for the Prevention of Cruelty to Vegetables.

Like New Zealand, Uruguay has had a prosperous agricultural past, mainly from beef and wool, and set up a comprehensive social welfare system which it now has trouble supporting. The large state sector is in the process of being privatised.

Outside the airport we climbed into a taxi which took off spitting tyre-rubber and trailing smoke at a pace which almost exceeded the aircraft's landing speed. The wheels hardly met the road until we touched down at the front door of the hotel. If anyone has ever wondered where 30-year-old Mercedes and failed racing-car drivers retire to, the answer is quite possibly to be found among the taxi ranks at Montevideo Aeroporto.

The Ibis Hotel was openly exposed to the wind. Outside, the halyards on a forest of flagpoles rattled continually in a stiff breeze that never let up and kept us awake all that night. This did nothing for our sanity or any lingering jetlag.

We were having trouble in South America adjusting to local eating times. It was 8.30 in the evening when we found the Alto Palermo restaurant one block behind the hotel. We peered inside like two starving orphans and the curious manager unbolted the doors. We'd arrived before the chef, so we drank a bottle of anorexic *vino tinto* merlot (vino but not much tinto) and waited for an hour. When our chicken finally arrived it had, at best, been waved over a barbecue flame.

It was 1 September next morning and the first day of spring

back home. We strolled down a chillingly windy and Sunday-quiet Avenida 18 de Julio, and photographed a boy who was perched on top of a pile of cardboard on the back of a cart drawn by a small bedraggled horse. Both could have done with a good feed. The boy was about 13 with a complexion turned dusky by life on the streets. Over well-worn jeans he had on a grimy padded jacket. His name was Daniel Soltero and he was helping his brother collect empties for recycling. I asked him what his dream was.

'What is the point of dreaming?' he said.

Other citizens who weren't already at church were being encouraged to go by way of booming messages broadcast through loudspeakers from roaming vans. We had an excuse. We had a plane to catch.

4 Brazil

Our flight to Sao Paulo was on Air Pluna. A group of Hassidic Jews, who had occupied one of the two counters for the excruciatingly long time that we were waiting to check in, was already on the plane as we edged down the aisle. Bunched around our seats they were busy stuffing into any space they could find what appeared to be the entire contents of a house.

Further down the plane were the members of a Brazilian band who were arguing and wildly waving their arms about as they tried to stow drums, guitars and assorted wind instruments in any locker that was left. We decided that fighting for our rights would be ill-advised and balanced our bags on our knees for the entire flight.

It was mid-evening when we touched down in Sao Paulo and we endured a 45-minute taxi ride to the Sofitel Sao Paulo on Rua Seno Madureina, a five-star hotel which, we had been assured, had a high-speed Internet connection. It had nothing of the sort.

Our stay was hardly long enough for us to pass opinion, but we agreed that a short stay is probably long enough in Sao Paulo, which is Brazil's industrial powerhouse. In the late 19th century the coffee boom brought massive immigration to the area from Italy, Portugal, Spain and, in the 1920s, from Japan. Brazil has the largest population of Japanese outside of Japan and two million of them live in Sao Paulo alone.

The city's attraction is not its beauty but the possibility of work. We were there on a Monday morning and the industrial smog, which was already heavy with pungent, chemical, brain-swelling odours, dimmed the sight of the ugly industrial buildings. Now the world's third largest metropolis, Sao Paulo attempts to support over 18 million people and about three trees. James said it looked like a scene from *Blade Runner* – chaotic, hideous and rather sinister. Nor were the people particularly cheerful. At the airport on the way out we asked five families if we could photograph their children for our children's book and got a sullen 'No, no, no, no, no' in reply.

5 Paraguay

Our arrival in Asunción was heralded by a military band playing on the tarmac. This was obviously not for us. We walked jauntily through the terminal and, stuffed into the oldest taxi on the rank, set off for town. The car travelled smoothly enough but appeared to have no brakes. The driver used his gears to slow himself down and stopped outside the hotel by running into the curb.

We were staying at the Excelsior Hotel and from the moment we stepped inside we liked it. The interior with its dark timber panels was grand but welcoming. The staff joked with us as they showed us to our suite, which was big enough to accommodate a whole tribe of Hassidic Jews. When you spend a lot of time cooped up in aeroplanes, space is attractive.

The city is laid out with leafy tree-lined avenues leading to a central Plaza de los Heros which is surrounded by Parisian-style buildings. Sitting on the steps of an attractive marble edifice was an appealing-looking girl of about nine. We mimed to a rather gruff old woman, who turned out to be her grandmother, that we'd like to take a photograph. The girl's mother, who had a smattering of English, then joined us and relayed our request to grandma, who immediately became director/producer. She hurried us off to the nearby Arts School and up five flights of stairs to a classroom. A worn case was hauled from a cupboard and she extracted a glowing violin and thrust it into the arms of the girl.

The star's name was Gianina Alexandra Klein Adorna and she said, with a side-long glance towards her *abuela* (grandmother), that her dream was to be a notable violin player. I don't think she had much choice.

6 Bolivia

The flight to Santa Cruz and on to La Paz was aboard a Fokker 100, which neither of us had ever flown in before. It was a small plane similar in shape to a DC9 with rear jet engines and low-mounted wings.

It was after landing in Santa Cruz that we had our first crisis. We'd begun to congratulate ourselves on our ability to keep our gear together when we discovered the minute we disembarked that we'd left our camera on the plane. Danny, the station manager for Tam Air, wouldn't hear of us going back on board to collect it. We could only stand and watch as the Fokker and our camera took off smoothly in the direction of Cochabamba in central Bolivia. Danny assured us that the plane was scheduled to return two hours later.

'Your camera will be okay,' Danny grinned confidently.

No doubt it would be, but in whose hands?

Somewhat grumpily, James and I retired to the Cargas Bar upstairs to drink a consoling beer and wait. Three hours later, Danny appeared with his mate Jimmy. They were both grinning triumphantly. Danny had our camera clutched in both hands, holding it out to us like a sacrificial offering. There was much handshaking and back-patting. Danny and Jimmy had their photograph taken holding our record book, looking very pleased with themselves.

The flight to La Paz was still three hours away, so we jumped into the back seat of the first cab on the rank to take us to town. The ageing vehicle pulled out from the curb but something was not quite right. The driver was in what should have been the passenger seat but he was gripping the steering wheel in front of him, the shaft of which disappeared into the glove box. All of the dials, none of which worked, were on the opposite side of the dashboard from where they were supposed to be; and where the steering wheel and the foot pedals should have been were two gaping holes. It was a DIY conversion Bolivian-style. Marco the driver found our concern amusing. He believed that the white line in the centre of the road was there as a steering guide. If he drove with two wheels on either side of it he couldn't go wrong.

'I have the choice of driving in either lane,' he explained – a choice which he executed often and with alarming nonchalance.

We had already travelled around 16,000 kilometres on this journey and so far it was not the flights that had caused us any concern. It was the taxi rides. The few kilometres that we covered in Marco's taxi to downtown Santa Cruz provided us with more life-threatening situations than all the others put together.

Through narrow dirty and polluted streets and a gridlock of traffic he took us to Plaza 24th September, which was animated by people milling around the food vendors, playing chess, promenading or standing in clusters earnestly debating politics and sport.

One of South America's poorest countries, Bolivia has become threadbare through an impotent economy and massive unemployment. But the people in the plaza seemed to be cheerfully making the best of things.

We flew from Santa Cruz to La Paz with Lloyd Aero Boliviano in an ancient 727-200. Our confidence for a safe delivery was not boosted by bolts rolling down the aisle and some alarming rattles.

Landlocked Bolivia sits astride the sky-piercing peaks of the Andes which, from the air, lend it a rugged magnificence. Al Alto, the airport for La Paz, is situated on the Altiplano, a plateau which is an incredible 4200 metres above sea level. This was the first time I had been in a plane that had to ascend in order to land.

Back in Santa Cruz, James had decided to wear shorts because the weather was warm and sunny. It was a decision he now regretted. When we landed at Al Alto it was nine o'clock at night and the temperature was seven degrees Celsius. I caught him eyeing the thick alpaca blankets worn by the small gathering of Indians outside the terminal.

The other thing we discovered as we left the plane was that something was definitely wrong with our energy levels. At that altitude, which was over 1400 metres higher than the summit of New Zealand's highest mountain, our bodies felt like lead. It took an incredible effort to move at all and we could execute the simplest tasks only in slow motion, as if we'd been darted with a paralysing drug.

There was a surreal quality, too, about the spectacular taxi ride down to La Paz, the highest city in the world. The business and wealthy residential areas are at the base of a deep canyon. Steep streets climb up from there to the high terraced sides of the valley which is where most of the Indian population lives.

The night was crystal-clear and a heavy coating of stars

merged with the lights from the Indian houses that swarmed over the precipitous slopes on either side of us. An ancient tape deck strapped to the dashboard was playing Handel's *Water Music*. The music, the lights and the effect of the altitude swam around our heads like some bizarre hallucination.

As we climbed out of the taxi when we reached the hotel, things became even more bizarre. Standing up made the world spin and we staggered into the Camino Real Hotel barely able to keep upright. The staff, who had gathered for our arrival, looked understanding as if staggering guests were nothing abnormal. We felt appalling and fell into the bar where we ordered two Pisco sours, the local apéritif, and then dragged ourselves to bed for four hours' restless and unrefreshing sleep.

At five-thirty the wake-up call had us stumbling around in silence trying to get organised to drag ourselves out the door and back into a taxi back to the airport. I'd woken up with a gut-wrenching nausea and a head that felt as if it was encased in concrete. It was like the hangover from hell.

The flight to Lima in Peru was leaving at 8.40 a.m. At the airport I was in worse working order. I threw up on the staircase in a desperate shuffle for the toilet and ended up with my head in a basin relieving myself of what felt like three nights' dinner. During this unlovely performance the bathroom attendant, a gnome of a man with rat-like teeth, gazed at me solemnly. When I finally straightened up, he rolled his eyes in an exasperated gesture and began cleaning up. I gave him $US5 and a reason to smile as I ambled out of the toilets trying to pretend that the mess on the stairs belonged to somebody else.

I yearned to be back into the pressurised aircraft cabin but the flight was delayed an hour. James and I found a corner in the terminal where we could sit and feel sorry for ourselves. When we finally climbed onto the Taca Airbus A319 there was another 30-minute delay while we waited for passengers on an incoming aircraft.

The two things that will always stay in my mind from that take-off, when it finally came, are the glorious feeling as the pressure began to rise and glorious sight of Lake Titicaca below us surrounded by reed-rich lagoons. Shared by Bolivia and Peru, the lake is the largest in South America and at 3812 metres is the highest navigable body of water in the world. The local Uru Indians live in little houses on floating islands, which are both made out of the lake's totora reeds.

As we travelled northwest across Peru we looked down on the pinched peaks and wrinkled flanks of vast mountain ranges divided by valleys filled with soft white cloud.

This was our first flight on Taca, a great little airline that started up only two years ago. The crew were fascinated by our journey and told the pilot. Captain Alfredo invited us up onto the flight deck and signed the record book. James thanked him and remarked, 'I didn't think I'd get to see a cockpit again after September 11.'

'Anything is possible in South America,' Alfredo said.

It isn't often in these commercial times that as you disembark the captain and co-pilot cheerily wave at you from the cockpit. We had seven more Taca flights ahead of us. We hoped at least one of them would be with Captain Alfredo and his crew.

CHAPTER THREE

SOUTH America, NORTH

 Peru

Our first impression of Lima was undoubtedly influenced by the thick grey haze that blanketed the city. The place was shabby and in need of maintenance and a good lick of paint. Large buildings were encased in rolls of vicious-looking wire as if they were prisons. Later in the day, in the Miraflores district from the top of high cliffs on the coastline, we looked down on surf beaches and parapenters soaring on the updraughts of an onshore breeze. Tucked into the cliff face were restaurants and shopping malls crammed with local sybarites.

On the way back to the airport the next day, Alahandro, the driver, a distinguished-looking man with hair streaked with grey, told us our opinion of Lima was wrong. 'You have not stayed long enough,' he said. 'It is a wonderful place. Two hours' drive

Captain Alfredo to Peru.

east of here there is good skiing. For hundreds of miles on either side of Lima there are very beoodiful beaches where you can swim and fish and the climate is beoodiful.'

'What about inflation?' I asked.

'Low,' he said, 'and only 20 percent unemployment. Twelve years go Lima was dangerous like Colombia. You heard of Sendero Luminoso? You see the wire everywhere? That tells you what it was like. It's okay now.' Sendero Luminoso (Shining Path) was a guerrilla group in the 1980s and 90s whose brutal activities killed 23,000 Peruvians and caused massive damage to the economy.

'Now we have democracy,' said Alahandro, as if he had conceived the idea himself. He had two sons. Both were doctors now working in Brazil and he was proud that he'd been able to educate them in a country of limited opportunities. 'For so many, education is an impossible dream,' he said.

We left Peru through the Jorge Chavez Airport, named after a famous air-force pilot who died in a plane crash.

8 Ecuador

The flight from Lima to Quito gave us another astonishing view of the Andes. Ecuador's landscape, which includes 30 active volcanoes, is almost as volatile as its political scene. The highlight was the descent into Quito where from the starboard window we could see a clear view of snow-capped Mt Cotopaxi (Moon Throne) which, at 5896 metres, is the highest active volcano in the world. It seemed just a wing-length away and it was comforting to know that it last erupted in 1877. Ecuador's most famous spot, the Galapagos Islands, was not on our flight path.

A sunny day clear of smog allowed us to see the neat grid of Quito, which is almost on the equator in a narrow valley surrounded by bare mountains. It is 2800 metres above sea level, which after our experience at La Paz made me very apprehensive about getting out of the plane. We left the aircraft gingerly, waiting to be hit by the staggers but the only thing I noticed was a bit of light-headedness.

Our taxi driver's name was Edwin Español and because he spoke a little English we booked him for a tour that afternoon. The best thing we did was to visit Museo de Sitio Inti-nan, an outdoor museum that through interactive displays outlined the earth's physical characteristics at the equator. Within two metres of the equator we were shown how water in the northern hemisphere goes down the plug hole clockwise, in the southern goes down anti-clockwise, and right on the equator goes straight down. On the equator we could also balance an egg on a nail head because of the greater pull of gravity.

For the children's book we photographed Jose, a boy of about 12 dressed in native costume who was demonstrating weaving with brightly coloured wool. I couldn't get him to smile but after the camera was safely stowed, he sidled up to us and grinned, displaying two rows of appallingly rotten teeth.

Edwin told us the boy's story. His father had died when he was small and his mother lived a long way away so the people of this village looked after him. His dream was to be a teacher but he hadn't been to school yet. I gave him $US20 and pointed to his teeth, but obviously it would cost a lot more to have them fixed. Not for the first time after we had just photographed a child, I left feeling inordinately inadequate.

Edwin filled our heads with 'facts' about Ecuador which were probably close to the truth. 'About a quarter of the population is Indian,' he said. 'They live in the mountains with flocks of sheep and have no power or wealth. The mestizos are the ones that have made big money from oil but it does not go any further than their own pockets. The unemployment is about 40 percent.'

Being a New Zealander I've always connected Ecuador with bananas – both the Bonita variety and Chiquita brand names. Amazingly I had never connected that in Spanish, bonita is beautiful and chiquita is small.

9 Colombia

Later that day we boarded an aircraft for the short flight to Bogotá. The passage through Customs had been extremely slow, due not to the thoroughness of security but to the Ecuadorian Customs official who was chatting up a voluptuous young woman. He laboriously filled out her forms, periodically pausing to cast a lascivious glance in the direction of her curves. It was lust (his, not ours) that caused us to be last to the departure gate.

We were flying on Avianca, the national airline of Colombia. Everyone knows about the perils of life in Colombia – the cocaine barons, drug cartels, emerald dealing, FARC rebels and guerrilla fighters. We were surprised that the crew were not wearing bulletproof vests and were neither cringing victims nor emboldened criminals.

Thania Raminez, Eldorado airport, Bogotá, Colombia.

It was also a surprise to find as we descended to Bogotá that the countryside reminded us of parts of New Zealand – a green, rolling plateau with lush pastures dotted with grazing horses and Friesian cows. Given Bogotá's safety record, and for the benefit of our families and Mike Henry Travel Insurance, we elected to stay in the transit lounge.

Back on the rather mature Aeropostal Boeing 727-200, we sat for another hour. We received no explanation for the delay but from the aircraft's window I could see a team of mechanics working away at something under the belly. Every now and then they emerged, gathered in a huddle, waved their arms around and disappeared again. It seemed to me that the guy who eventually signed off the paperwork did so with a resigned kind of shrug, and as the engines were gunned the mechanics looked back at the plane uncertainly. We half-expected to explode on take-off.

Below us Bogotá was not the shot-to-hell cesspit we'd imagined, but an attractive city with parks and greenery and a sophisticated and expansive central area of Spanish colonial architecture and soaring skyscrapers. We were sorry that we hadn't spent the night.

But some things are better left as planned. Twenty-four hours later we heard that while we'd huddled at the airport, the main street in downtown Bogotá was besieged by a hail of gunfire that left two people dead.

10 Venezuela

The flight attendant on the national Aeropostal Airline was an arrogant, gum-chewing female from Colombia who plonked down something that passed for food in front of us as if she were feeding a trough of pigs. Aeropostal, loosely translated, means postcard. It was nothing to write home about.

We'd mentioned Caracas to a few people and they had implored us to avoid it. The discovery of oil has turned the country from an economic backwater into the richest country in South America, but that has done nothing for the country's poor except to widen the gap.

Even the road from the airport into Caracas was not for the faint-hearted. It was a very steep ascent, which at eight o'clock on a Friday night was bumper to bumper with what looked like the collection of a motor museum – ancient cars, trucks and motorbikes in need of repair and belching clouds of smoke. Caracas is notorious for its web of motorways, frenzied traffic, constant traffic jams and heavy pollution. Our driver handled the mayhem by disregarding anything blocking the road and zigzagging from one lane to another, judging gaps in the traffic down to the last millimetre.

So it was a white-knuckle drive in through the inner city where a thoroughly unsavoury lot were gathering to celebrate, we presumed, the fact that it was Friday night.

The city is a mix of impressive modern architecture, parks and sculptures, and impoverished shanties that creep up the surrounding hillsides. We scurried into the lobby of the

President Hotel where the receptionist received us with such aloof indifference that we discussed changing accommodation. Perhaps she thought we were drug runners.

From the moment we touched down to the moment we left, the citizens of Caracas were surly and unhelpful. The city was crazy with cars and dangerous to walk around after dark. But there was one thing to celebrate in Caracas. Venezuela was the 10th nation we'd visited in 10 days. We had already travelled 19,513 kilometres on nine different airlines and were still in good shape. Only two nations to go, Suriname and Guyana, and we would have been to every nation in South America.

But before then we would have a day on the Caribbean Island of Trinidad.

11 Trinidad and Tobago

Our departure from Caracas was in character, in that the ground staff were tight-lipped and terse. The small West Indian Airlines Dash 8-300 we boarded was the first aircraft we'd flown in with propellers. It was an absolute joy, for no other reason than we were escaping Caracas at 400 km/h. Trinidad and its quieter neighbour, Tobago, lie off the Orinoco river delta of north-eastern Venezuela. Beaches and coral reefs rim both islands, but they haven't always been idyllic. Forty-three percent of the population are descendents of African slaves and 40 percent are descended from Indians brought in as indentured labourers to work on the sugar estates after slavery was abolished. This was also the home of the steel drum and the king of calypso, Mighty Sparrow, as well as the writers VS and Shiva Naipaul.

As soon as we landed at Piarco Airport near Port of Spain, we felt at home on this island of carnival, calypso and cricket, with its tropical rainforest setting and joyous people. The rhythmic island dialect took a while to adjust to, but at least the signs were in English. As we emerged from the terminal we were confronted by a barrage of taxi drivers. We tried to avoid them by walking right past but a cheerful voice boomed out, 'Hey maan, where you goin'?'

That's how we met Cleaver Mitchell, a young man with the physique of a going-to-seed rugby forward and skin like buffed ebony. With a name like that he was not the sort of fellow you'd mess with, not even to beat his fare down. We could have bought the vehicle for his initial price but it plummeted when we said we would hire him for a tour of the island the next day.

He took us around the eastern side of the island, winding through tangled trees and vines and simple villages, then over a range of mountains to Maracas Bay where it seemed as if half the population of Trinidad was at the beach. At a small thatched stall Cleaver insisted that we try bake 'n' shark, the local delicacy of fried shark in a light bun, with delicious lashings of pineapple, tomato and a secret dressing that was heavy on chilli.

Back in the taxi we cruised around the world's largest round-about (five kilometres in circumference) encompassing the parkland known as the Savannah. Cleaver pointed out the home of cricketing legend Brian Lara and the stone prison where West African slaves were kept before their auction. I asked him if the West Africans, Indians and Chinese in Trinidad got on together. 'Hey maan, they get on just fine,' he said. 'Us Africans were brought here by the English – they just forgot to take us home.'

We were en route to a very forgettable bird-watching excursion on Coroni swamp. The tour had already started when we got there, so we missed seeing a snake and an anteater. But we did see flocks of scarlet ibis which, James hissed at me, are pests in Brisbane. We were sitting in a small, open boat in the middle of a swamp, being targeted by a battalion of mosquitoes. This was not our idea of a good time.

12 Suriname

We left Port of Spain at 11:30 p.m. and arrived at Zanderij Airport at 1 a.m. An enthusiastic taxi driver leant against the barred window of the immigration office as we were completing the visa application forms. 'Taxi?' he enquired in a squeaky whine. The timbre of his voice, he said, was due to an excessive quantity of bad whisky consumed 48 hours before. We believed the whisky story but not the timing.

The road to our accommodation, which happily wasn't far, was a pothole with bitumen surrounds. I don't think it had been touched since the Dutch left in 1975.

We were both anticipating a brief but good night's sleep, but hope was shattered when we pulled up at the accommodation recommended by the Surinamese Tourist Office, the Guesthouse Zanderij. A pack of mangy hounds circled us for 10 minutes until the proprietor emerged from around the half-lit, partially-constructed east wing of the concrete building to show us to our rooms. Mr Andrew was a slight Surinamese man of West African descent. He looked tousled and sleepy but wrung his hands together at the prospect of guests.

One glance around the interior and we gave the hotel an All Nations Quest star-rating of one, on the basis that it was still standing. To describe the bedrooms as tired would be an understatement. But the rate was $US25 so we decided to lash out and have a room each. The first one I was offered had a narrow single bed in it with a bare, grubby foam mattress and no bed linen. The next was only a slight improvement. Downstairs there was no refrigeration, no beer, no bottled water, no coffee and plenty of cockroaches.

Mr Andrew was at pains to point out the scale of the planned renovations. 'When we have finished it will be finest hotel in the country,' he said, raising his hands skyward as if his vision were already true. None of those plans involved a bulldozer.

The next morning James was woken by a large monkey performing jungle yoga in the tree outside the tiny window of his room. It was a large browny-red animal with very long arms. James was ecstatic. Here he was in the wild surrounded by jungle animals. If he'd had a pith helmet he would have donned it before he rushed down the corridor to tell me of his find. We peered out my window and the first thing I saw was the leg rope. The poor creature was Mr Andrew's tethered pet.

As the room rate did not include soap or towels or any other nod in the direction of cleanliness, and as there was no sign of any form of sustenance, we paid the bill, wished Mr Andrew well with his renovations and fled back down the pothole to the airport.

It was frustrating, but perhaps for the best, that tight flight connections did not allow us a visit to the country's capital Paramaribo, which was 58 kilometres from the airport. Like the whole country, the city is not particularly stable: the US consulate warned that violence was frequent. But we would have liked to have seen the city's collection of churches, synagogues, Hindu temples and mosques that reflect the ethnic mix of people who settled here under Dutch rule.

For the sake of Suriname's future in tourism we don't propose to put Guesthouse Zanderij forward as an example of the general standard of accommodation. Maybe future guests, AR (after renovations), will have a completely different story to tell.

13 Guyana

DC 9s still fly the uncrowded skies between Suriname and Guyana. We first saw one of these geriatric aeroplanes on the tarmac at Zanderij Airport after a long sweltering battle through check-in. The thought of boarding a plane of such a great age was causing me a certain amount of inner turmoil.

'Verwelkomen,' said the attendant, beaming encouragingly.

'She smileth too much,' I thought.

In fact, the 45-minute flight was great. At last we saw real South American rainforest, thousands of hectares of it spreading out as far as the eye could see – a dense, dark, textured covering moulded to the hilly contours of the land.

Ninety-five percent of Guyana is still covered in rainforest, much of it so impenetrable that the country's population lives along the coastal strip and spreads inland only along the banks of the Demara River. Somewhere to the south in those forests was the site of Jim Jones' cult settlement Jonestown, where he and more than 900 followers committed mass suicide in 1978.

In its heyday Georgetown must have been a pleasant, thriving port town, but from what we saw on our journey to town this was a long time ago. Known as British Guiana until independence in 1966, Guyana, the only English-speaking country in South America, was now bedevilled by racial problems and a wretched economy. Early Dutch settlers had drained the marshy swamps where the city is sited and built a comprehensive canal and dyke system to keep the sea at bay. The once-sturdy buildings were now disintegrating, held together with random bits of timber and tin. The whole place looked neglected and forlorn. Of the grand old buildings left by the British and Dutch, we saw only two that looked to be in a reasonable state.

The walled Meridien Hotel divorced us from the surrounding city. Our taxi driver, Roy Man, told us not to venture onto the streets any time of day or night. 'There are killings all the time,' he said. 'The United States repatriated 150 of the toughest of its Guyanese criminals from American jails a while ago and now they roam our streets creating havoc. Eleven policemen have been killed in the last three months and four high-ranking officers have been arrested for corruption.'

A youthful-looking black man, inscrutable behind his dark

glasses, Roy was one cool dude; tall, lithe and fast-thinking. In town he drove with the windows up and doors locked. On the way back to the airport that next morning he must have felt safer because he turned up the music and hung his elbow out the open window.

He was our last South American taxi driver. We had survived the lot.

CHAPTER FOUR

carıввean

14 Grenada

Seen from the air, the thickly-forested volcanic peaks of Grenada rose sharply to a brilliant sky as an azure sea nudged at the glistening white beaches and coral reefs.

Our taxi driver to town was Algie McDonald. 'I am a descendant of a Scottish great-grandfather and a West African great-grandmother,' he announced grandly. We could see little that was Gaelic in his shiny black skin and thin sprinkle of peppercorn curls. He smiled to reveal a full row of dazzling white teeth. 'My father,' he added, 'is a nutmeg farmer.'

Algie drove us around this pretty island, which Christopher Columbus named after Granada in Spain, and through the streets of St George's where small colourful houses spilled down to the deep blue-green waters of the bay.

We were staying at the Blue Horizon cottages, a three-star outfit which we felt involved one celestial image too many, and in the evening ate in the restaurant which was touted as above-average, although nothing but the price was of a high standard.

15 St Vincent and the Grenadines

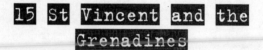

On the Caribbean Star island-hopper next morning we almost lost the pilot. The hostess had locked the door and was half-way through her safety speech when there was a banging from the outside and a faint and plaintive cry, 'Let me in'. Suppressing a giggle, the hostess finished her instruction then calmly turned and opened the door. In climbed the first officer muttering and looking sheepish as he slunk towards the cockpit. The door was shut with a plunk, the propellers fired up, and we departed.

There was a black cloud the colour of tyre smoke over St Vincent and the aircraft took up a holding pattern to the west of it until the storm passed. Thirty minutes later we dropped steeply from the sky for a perfect three-point landing at ET Joshua International Airport.

Weather disruptions like that are very common in the Caribbean. The little Dash 8s that hop from one island to the next were run more like bus transport than air services. One plane flew every day to four or five islands and then returned a few hours later. When it landed, its offside engine was left running while passengers debouched, the luggage was offloaded and the next lot loaded up. Then they were off again. The whole procedure took only about 20 minutes.

We were welcomed to St Vincent by wide smiles and nods from the immigration officers, but from then on we experienced the sort of indifference that was to become typical of the Caribbean. It was disconcerting that all through the region the people who essentially put the largest quantity of food on the table, tourists, were so often treated in a brusque and off-hand manner.

In the muggy heat of late afternoon we sat on the patio of the Ocean Rise Restaurant on the foreshore of Kingstown harbour while the owner, Sylvanie Lewis, a highly-opinionated dark-skinned woman, pointed out in a loud slapping voice that she was not too happy with the way the island had been occupied in the past. 'In our Botanic Gardens,' she said, 'there is a breadfruit tree which is descended from one brought from Tahiti by Captain Bligh in 1792. He grew breadfruit to feed the African slaves in the sugar plantation. Not a great success. The Africans preferred bananas. Two thirds of the island population are those slaves' descendants. They still like bananas.'

St Vincent is one of the poorest of the Caribbean nations. We trudged around the centre of the city, which looked dishevelled and neglected. Hawkers and vendors roamed the streets and many people begged for money and cigarettes. The cataclysmic events in New York the previous September had affected Caribbean tourism badly.

In the early morning James walked up a hill behind the hotel and looked down on the thick tangle of forest. The strains of Bob Marley and the Wailers floated up from a small, unpainted wooden house. He watched white egrets settle on the backs of grazing cattle and a few mangy dogs foraging around the roadsides. A small bus ground up the slope dropping off schoolchildren. It was the sort of Caribbean setting that would become very familiar over the next few days.

16 Barbados

The next short hop was with LIAT Airlines and from the Bridgetown airport we were transported to the Grand Barbados Hotel, which was a mixture of pleasant staff and past-their-best rooms. Later we sauntered through the rambling downtown area of Bridgetown among buildings that were, like us, worn down by the rigours of a tropical climate.

Among the Caribbean nations, Barbados is one of the most prosperous. Its pale beaches lure tourists on cruise ships to enjoy the nightclubs and the familiar amenities mixed with a bit of exotica. But the surly rudeness of the locals here did not endear us to the island one little bit. We were made to feel like unwelcome intruders.

There are still remnants of colonial occupation of the island which was once so British it was dubbed 'Little England'. In Trafalgar Square, a statue of Lord Nelson takes pride of place; there are small Gothic stone churches; and in one shop a portrait of Queen Liz hung above the counter. Then of course there's cricket, the foremost religion of the nation. Barbados is said to boast more world-class cricketers for its population than any other place in the world, and cricketing hero Sir Frank Worrell is depicted on the Barbados five-dollar bill.

17 St Lucia

Next morning the hotel doorman called up the only taxi on the rank to take us to the airport. The van approached in slow motion and when it finally arrived at the door, the driver, hunched and stiff with age, took so long to get out of his van that we had ourselves and our gear on board by the time his feet had touched the ground. He then had to go through the equally slow and painful process of trying to get back into his seat. The doorman lifted him up, deftly tucking his dragging bits behind the wheel.

'The airport please,' I said. 'Do you remember how to get there?'

His spectacles were the thickness of a glass brick, which didn't concern us until we noticed he was stopping dead every time something came within 100 metres of the car. The poor fellow was also deaf. It took several minutes to get his attention to implore him to speed up so that we might get to the airport in the same month that we'd set out. His great age, however, did not diminish the speed at which he grasped the fare.

As we hurried out over the tarmac, we were suddenly ordered to one side by police so that Prime Minister Owen Arthur of Barbados could precede us to the plane. He was a short man who sported a number-two haircut and the corpulent figure and contented countenance of the well-fed.

At Vigie Airport on St Lucia while queuing to leave the plane, I found myself standing next to PM Arthur, who was still seated. He was reading the sports page of the day's newspaper which bore the terrible news that the Australian cricket team had just beaten the West Indies. He looked disconsolate. 'Never mind, mate,' I said. 'I'm from New Zealand and we can't beat them either.'

At St Lucia we found the friendly isle. Despite being larger in area than Barbados, it has a much smaller population and is less geared to tourism. As a consequence, the people are charmingly polite. The wooden French colonial buildings of Castries are spic and span. Most of the town burned down in 1948 and had to be rebuilt, so although the buildings look authentically old-style most of them are new. Elias George, our taxi driver, told us that a cigarette butt in a tailor's shop started the inferno.

He drove us up a steamy road to the Green Parrot Hotel perched high above Port Castries. As we entered the foyer an aroma that gave new meaning to the term 'mothballed' overwhelmed us.

'Keeps the place fresh,' said the desk attendant.

We liked the hotel. Our room was large and airy with bright floral décor. A tangle of power lines was the only thing that marred a sensational view over the bay.

St Lucia is a spear-shaped island dominated by two dramatic

jungle-covered peaks where brilliantly coloured birds of paradise and the fer-de-lance pit viper live. The rest of the island is rural and covered with a mix of jungle and untidy banana plantations with small villages scattered around the coastline.

Shortly after we arrived it started raining in a tropical sort of way. Heavy drops drummed down on the hot earth and in minutes everything was soaked. It was still raining next morning, but we were determined to tour the island with Elias even though we could see only a few metres on either side of the car. He quoted us $50 for a two-hour drive. 'Forty dollars,' I said, 'and every time you let someone try to sell us something it's a dollar off.' He laughed good-naturedly. 'Yeah man, it's okay.'

He took us to the northern tip of the island and up a steep road that writhed up a mountain and was so narrow that crashing into any vehicles coming in the opposite direction was almost inevitable. It was Friday, 13 September, a date that could only increase our chances of calamity. I was right. The crash did not directly involve us but a minibus and a car just ahead crunched together head on.

Such incidents were obviously common. St Lucia's one-way road system is one-way – whatever way you happen to be going – and the sides of the road were littered with rusting car corpses gradually being claimed by the creeping jungle.

Calabash trees grow around the island and breadfruit trees are everywhere, but back at the Green Parrot the menu offered the choice of some rather startling dishes: 'stuffed pussy in season' or 'filet of bird with bacon'. We never did discover what they actually were.

18 Antigua and Barbuda

We hit our first real snag. We were meant to be flying to the island of Dominica but the violent weather forced the pilot to fly on to

Antigua. Many passengers remonstrated indignantly as if the airline's staff had deliberately organised the storm.

'How fokkin ridiculous, man,' bellowed a pugnacious-looking fellow standing next to me. I didn't argue. Another man, a little smaller but just as wild-looking, rattled his dreadlocks and proclaimed that it was a conspiracy to thwart his personal plans. Dr Shaman, an Indian psychiatrist, moaned that it was his birthday and his wife was preparing a special welcome for him. 'She is waiting in a pink negligee with a bottle of champagne,' he lamented. 'But I am in Antigua and she is in Dominica.'

We hung around the airport like a mob of lost sheep until it was announced that no further flights would be going to Dominica that day and we would be transported to the nearby Beachcomber Resort to be given complimentary rooms and meals. The hotel was no more than a holding pen, but our budget had already taken a battering from the rapacious over-pricing in many parts of the Caribbean, so a free night was welcomed.

We sat at the bar for three hours and drank beer at inflated prices while our room, we finally decided, was being 'constructed', not prepared.

At the bar that night we met Tom, an Englishman seeking refuge from what he described as 'wrongful arrest' back home; Richard, also a Londoner, who was there to explore the diving spots; and Camalla, who worked for Radio DBS in Dominica. Camalla was a long-limbed, stunning-looking girl who had been Miss Dominica two years ago. She was insistent that we gave an interview on Radio DBS during our brief stop at Dominica airport the next day.

Incessant caterwauling music from the hotel bar that night thwarted our attempts to sleep and by six the next morning we were in the air looking back at the island which, for a change, was dry and sparsely covered in scrub.

19 Dominica

There was a bit of excitement as we descended to Dominica on a LIAT Dash 8, 40 minutes after take-off. The Melville Hall airport runway is at right angles to a beach, which is fine if the wind is offshore. Rain belted down on the rugged jungle and thick cloud swirled down to 300 feet. The descent was exhilarating – if you like that sort of thing – as we banked and swayed through densely vegetated valleys to get into position for landing into the wind. There was an audible sigh of relief from the passengers as the plane settled into its chocks on solid ground.

The downpour continued. The propellers kept turning and the captain suggested that, because there were only four umbrellas, we should wait out the worst of it before we attempted the 50-metre dash to the terminal. With rain two days out of every three, the island has around 2500 mm of rain a year and this was nothing unusual.

Before we flew back to Antigua and on to St Kitts on Caribbean Star airlines, I had time to do Camalla's interview for the local radio station but first I had to buy a phone card in a small shop which, with no fan and no air conditioning, was an inferno. The large exhausted-looking women behind the counter waved her hand at me and said, 'Go get it yourself, man. I am light in the head today.'

On the back of the card was the picture of Elizabeth Pampo Isreal and underneath it her message: 'Live simply. Stop fighting.' Ma Pampo was said by locals to be the second-oldest person living in the world. The granddaughter of an African slave, she was born on 27 January 1875, which made her 128 years old. I doubted if the card-seller was going to live that long.

A smiling Dominican called Wathley Rose checked us in. 'I don't think you'll make the connecting flight to St Kitts,' he grinned cheerfully. 'There's only 20 minutes between planes and it won't be enough.' We resigned ourselves to cooling our heels in Antigua waiting for the next available flight to St Kitts.

Ten minutes later Wathley Rose tracked us down again. 'Hey, get your skates on,' he said. 'We're sending the flight early so you can get your connection. All the other passengers have checked in.'

James and I grabbed our bags and raced past the Customs officials who were obligingly cursory in their inspection. Wathley had radioed ahead to the Antiguan authorities and arranged for us to be met for the transfer. We had come across a lot of Dominicans in the Caribbean and without fail they had been cordial and kind-hearted. We would have liked to have spent more time on their island which is poor but richly endowed with goodwill.

20 St Kitts and Nevis

It was the 18th day of the journey and St Kitts was our 20th nation. Only five passengers got off the plane at Robert L Bradshaw Airport. The island is a sleepy place and one of the least exciting in the Caribbean. My interchange with the immigration officer was typical:

'How long are you planning to stay in St Kitts?'

'One day.'

'Why only one day?'

'We are establishing a record for visiting every country in the world.'

At this point he looked at us as if we were drug smugglers with a good story. 'So which countries have you been to?'

'Antigua, Dominica, St Lucia, Barbados, St Vincent, Grenada, Guya . . .'

'Okay, okay.' Stamp, stamp. 'Go through,' accompanied by a dismissive wave of the hand.

Outside the terminal we hailed a taxi driven by Andrew. On the seven-minute trip into Basseterre we agreed to let him take us to the main attraction on St Kitts, Fort George on the bowl-shaped, volcanic cone of Brimstone Hill. The British built this extensive fortress in 1690 to try to recapture coastal Fort Charles from the French. Heavy cannons still faced out to the Caribbean Sea and from the ramparts we could see most of the island, which bristles with sugarcane. The Fort is now a Unesco world heritage site.

'No snakes now,' said Andrew. 'Mongooses were brought in to control them. The mongooses thrived, the snakes disappeared; now we kill the mongooses.'

James, the critter-lover of the two of us, was disappointed about the snakes. Despite the low odds, he spent his time at the fort trying to spot one.

Back at the Palms Hotel we received the Caribbean greeting ritual, which was only marginally better than that meted out to the mongooses. When the receptionist showed us to our room we warmed to her a little until we realised she was hanging around for a tip. She went unrewarded.

It was Sunday next day and out on the street it was like the *Marie Celeste* – hot and eerily still. Victorian stone-and-timber buildings trimmed with fancy latticework clustered around a roundabout called the Circus. The only performance that day was a couple of dawdling hens and a forlorn, hungover taxi driver slumped over the wheel of a clapped-out black taxi. This was not Andrew, who was no doubt at home planning his retirement from our payment for the ride to Brimstone Hill.

Along the streets were many small concrete pubs and rum houses – the Mango Tree, Red Bull and the Willie George. Patrons sat out on the steps where it was coolest to quaff their rum and beer.

St Kitts is an attractive island but battered palm trees and a thrice-rebuilt marina attest to the hurricanes that frequently rocket through. There are signs everywhere that warn: 'Disasters are swift and sudden. Be prepared.'

 21 Dominican Republic

Back at the airport we discovered that our flight to Puerto Rico was delayed, which meant we would miss our connection to the Dominican Republic where we'd intended to overnight.

At first the delay was two hours. That extended to six and finally the flight was cancelled. We rang and cancelled the hotel in Santo Domingo and sat down in the airport café for a snack. A small beer and pathetically small cheeseburger cost $NZ30. We ate feeling rather sour. Then another announcement blared out: a flight to DR would leave later that night. Oh, the joys of travel.

We transited through San Juan in Puerto Rico where the security was almost paranoid because the island is considered to be a gateway to the US. Our luggage was screened four times. Our shoes were removed and then we were asked for IDs at random intervals as we were making our way to the plane.

We eventually arrived in Santo Domingo at 11 that night. There was something warming and familiar about being among Spanish speakers again – we'd enjoyed the people of South America much more than we had those of the Caribbean. We drove past noisy and colourful restaurants and nightclubs and the town's youth hanging out around their cars, jigging around to loud merengue music. Along with salsa, this is the hottest music style in a nation where music, colour and dance are at the heart of the vivacious life. We stayed what little of the night was left at the Melia Santo Domingo hotel in the city centre, and in the morning cleared our emails to discover a message from Rolandro Altagracia, the brother of Pedro our New Zealand-based translator. Rolando, his sister Bianca Cabron, and her son had waited in vain at Santo Domingo Airport the night before for the arrival of our scheduled flight.

They came to the hotel for coffee. Rolando was a handsome man of slight build, his copper-coloured skin attesting to his European/African heritage. Both he and Bianco spoke good English. 'You must come back and stay longer,' said Rolando, who had travelled by bus from Le Romona, his home town on the south coast, just to see us. 'We have beautiful beaches.'

Rolando was a computer engineer and Bianca worked as a marketing consultant. Many of their countrymen were not employed. 'Life can be a struggle here,' said Rolando, 'but people enjoy themselves.'

Columbus referred to this island of Hispaniola as 'the most beautiful island that man had ever seen'. Many people there believe that his body lies under the large, white cross-shaped structure that we passed on the way back to the airport. Rolando came with us along a highway that hugged the coastline and looked out on the glassy blue sea. Every now and then sprays of water shot into the air from blowholes in the rocks and waved in the breeze like gestures of farewell.

22 Haiti

Descending to Guy Malory airport at the other end of the island of Hispaniola, near Port-au-Prince, we looked down on countless ships beached on the shallows of the harbour. Drab, fragmented slum dwellings crowded the shore and stretched back into the hills as far as we could see.

Outside the airport terminal a clamouring wall of humanity pressed against an iron barrier. We pushed through the jostling throng like a couple of rugby loose forwards and fell into a taxi. The ride to our hotel shocked us. Most vehicles on the road were in need of a good panelbeater or mechanic, several were pocked with bullet holes, and many had loose and wobbling wheels. The main form of transport was brightly painted utes called taptaps in which passengers sat face-to-face on benches in the back. The roads were rutted, pot-holed, heaped with rubble and bordered by open sewers and shacks made of scraps of timber, cardboard and tin leaning against each other for support.

A stream of women balancing plastic cans or buckets on their heads wove through chickens, mangy dogs and squatting children towards a communal tap. (Only half the population of Haiti has access to clean water and only the elite has electricity.) Other people loitered, cooked and tinkered on the streets. They would do anything for money: 'I carry bags, please.' 'I show you where?' 'You take my picture?'

Haiti's main source of income is remittances from Haitians who live in the US. Some tourists come here for the beaches way north of Port-au-Prince, to which I imagine most are spirited off pretty quickly.

Road signs were few and far between, and those we did see were often twisted and battered. The few hoardings advertised Maggi soup, or Coronation Condensed Milk, King Kola and Pepsi. On a crumbling concrete wall a crudely painted notice read: 'No urine a qui por favour.' Please don't piss on the wall.

We were staying at the Kinam Hotel, which was in the Petionville area. Outside was a guard holding a sawn-off shotgun but inside was an oasis after the mayhem of the streets. The Kinam was three storeys high, set around a central courtyard dominated by a swimming pool. Ornate wooden screens and louvres gave the interiors privacy and allowed a cool breeze to enter. Best of all, as far as James was concerned, the bar sold a local beer called Prestige Haitian (Medal d'Or 2000) which was not only cheap but tasted extremely good. Our attempts to understand the Creole spoken by the West African barmen created much merriment.

Petionville is the posh district, largely built on the cool hills above the slums where the privileged mulattos (mixed-race) live with access to good restaurants and more upmarket shops: mulattos make up five percent of the population, and one percent of them own 44 percent of the wealth.

James got up early next morning and went for his walk up a wooded hill behind the hotel. A black family was climbing just ahead of him – a mother, an older daughter and three small children. All had some form of bucket filled with water on their heads. There were some very elegant homes on either side of the track, walled off from reality by bars and razor wire. They had large gardens and satellite dishes and electric garage doors. The contrast with the family trudging up the hill carrying their water supply on their heads along a rough track lined with rubbish demonstrated the deep division between rich and poor in Haiti.

On the lighter side, Haiti has a strong culture in music and art. Later in the day we walked down the Rue Metellus to Expressions Art Gallery. It was raining steadily and although most of the place looked as if it had been nuked, the gallery was in a modern building and displayed a large collection of the local art which is rich with bright colours and sensual in form. The gallery was owned by a man who said he was French, but went by the name of Habib Jiha. It was only in some of the paintings hung in his gallery that we saw any evidence of voodoo, the ritualistic sorcery which is still widely practised here alongside the rituals of the Roman Catholic faith. I bought a surreal painting of Haitians living out their lives inside the enlarged figure of a woman, which Habib packed in a cardboard cylinder for me to carry.

Despite the appalling state of Haiti's economy, its woeful infrastructure and the residue of brutal repression from the infamous Papa Doc and his thugs, the people were full of good cheer. The current leader is Jean Bertrand Aristide, a former slum priest about whom no one seemed willing to comment.

23 Bahamas

Security at the Haiti airport was intense. A mobile scanner had been mounted by American Airlines in a truck at the door that led to the tarmac and carry-on bags passed through it before passengers were allowed onto the plane. Amazingly, no one queried the fact that I was holding a cardboard cylinder about the right size for an automatic rifle.

At Miami we cleared US Immigration and sank onto comfortable seats in the departure lounge to relax until our flight to the Bahamas. Suddenly we were on full alert. On the TV screens CNN was warning of a tropical cyclone called Isidore which was, at that moment, battering the east coast of Jamaica, gathering in strength and heading for Cuba. So were we.

But we had a night in Nassau first. Driving to our hotel we were struck by how warm and balmy it was and how, after Haiti, everything was so orderly and clean.

And then I was struck by a thought that was not orderly at all. I had left my painting at the airport. How was I going to break the news to our insurer that within 24 hours I had bought and lost a painting?

At the hotel James took control. He rang lost luggage at the airport, discovered it was there and arranged for me to collect it on our way out the next day.

24 Jamaica

Back at the airport, automatic rifle/painting once again tucked under my arm, we boarded the American Airlines Boeing 737-800 which was to take us to Kingston, Jamaica. The atmosphere was tense. Isadore was on everybody's mind. 'Could you get us an update?' I asked the attendant. He looked around furtively.

'Unlikely we'll get into Kingston,' he whispered.

We took off into the wind and were advised to belt up and stay put. A few people tried to get to the toilets but the turbulence increased and they never made it. We watched them stagger back to their seats, frowning with the concentration of mentally crossing their legs.

The captain announced that the 737-800, being a very new plane, had the latest weather-tracking equipment and could easily fly around the worst of the weather. Seconds later, the plane plunged a couple of hundred feet. From that moment nobody, including the captain I imagine, believed a word of what he'd said.

In fact the descent into Kingston not only happened but, apart from the odd jolt, was uneventful despite the driving rain and zero visibility. In the seat behind us a woman was muttering incessantly. She had, it seemed, located a higher being than the pilot to get us onto land.

The rain came at us from all directions, including up. Even inside the terminal, large areas were awash. We battled our way to the exit and chose our taxi driver by a simple process: he already had our bags tucked under each arm. He was also a large man in a very small van but neither James nor I felt inclined to tell him that we might choose someone else.

'No problem, mun,' he assured us. 'Ah am a very careful driver.' This care lasted as far as the airport gates, whereupon he revved up like a kamikaze pilot and hurtled through the lakes of water that had formed across the unlit road.

I asked him how many people lived in Kingston.

'Aah dunno, mun.'

'Does everybody get on well in Jamaica?'

'Yaaas, mun.'

We passed a hotel outside which a forest of international flags battled the strong wind. 'We are going to every one of those countries.' I said. 'To every country in the world in 160 days.' I waited for an impressed response.

'Oh yaaas. Okay mun.'

And then we started on cricket and we couldn't stop him from talking all the way into town. We had gained respect. From then on 'yaaas mun' changed to 'Yes sir'.

We had intended to stay in Kingston for 22 hours but the plan was distorted by the reports that Havana, our stop next day, was bracing for Isidore. The storm was now a thousand kilometres off the coast of Jamaica and gathering strength. By the time it hit western Cuba it would be a category three, which meant wind speeds of up to 205 kilometres an hour and even higher gusts. Not the sort of weather to be flying around in. We decided to reroute and began enquiries. Our only options were back to the US or on to Panama City. COPA, Panama's national carrier, was the only airline still intending to fly the next day.

James had imagined that in Kingston he might stroll downtown and sit around with a few rastas in a square somewhere to smoke marijuana and play chess. It seemed unlikely. Venturing out into Kingston was not very practical. Not only was the town drowning but we'd been warned that crime made it dangerous.

However, the only dangerous part of our visit to Kingston was in the hotel laundry where a large notice on the wall informed us that we were using the equipment voluntarily and were responsible for any damage, injury or death. We turned on the washer with as much caution as members of a bomb squad.

Next morning we went straight out to the airport. The flight to Havana had been cancelled and the one to Panama City was full. We bought a ticket on stand-by. Two hours passed. We reported back to the COPA ticketing desk and were told that good fortune was shining on us. We had our seats.

As we climbed the steps of the B737-200, James and I congratulated ourselves for wheedling our way onto a full flight and attributed this success to our abundant charm. But inside we discovered there were more empty seats than were occupied. Perhaps a lot of people had decided not to fly.

35 CANADA

34 UNITED STATES OF AMERICA

29 MEXICO

30 CUBA

33 BELIZE

28 GUATEMALA   31 HONDURAS

27 EL SALVADOR   32 NICARAGUA

26 COSTA RICA   25 PANAMA

central and NOrTH AMERICA

25 Panama

In Panama I was, not for the last time, glad to have James. As soon as we landed at Panama City airport he started reorganising our route through Central America until the Internet café closed. He also managed to reserve us on a 6 a.m. flight to Costa Rica the next morning.

To give him more time to continue with the whole rescheduling of our Central American arrangements we stayed at the Riandes close to the airport. This did not excite our taxi driver, who had waited around for us for about two hours, but he calmed down when I offered him a few extra dollars.

Alas, Panama was nowhere near the cutting edge of IT. James made little headway until around midnight he phoned Ann Torstonson at Flight Centre in Auckland. In a few hours she had rebooked our entire Central American leg. The itinerary now went like this: Costa Rica, El Salvador, Guatemala, back to El Salvador, Mexico, Cuba, back to Mexico, Honduras through El Salvador (again), Nicaragua, Belize and back to San Salvador from where we would leave for New York. Confused? So were we. The pace had certainly picked up since those first days in South America and the Caribbean. This was no holiday.

In our room at the Riandes the strains of late-night merengue music drifted up from the bar. Heavy metal wouldn't have kept me awake. We had two hours left in which to sleep.

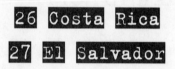

At the hideous hour of 4 a.m., I felt as if I'd just come out of an anaesthetic. My head was cotton-wool. My legs belonged to someone else and at the airport, every time a plane took off, the vibrations set off all the car alarms in the carpark. My world had taken on a very bizarre quality.

James, on the other hand, was in his element. He was still focussed on resetting the schedule and was scrabbling through bits of paper like a dog digging up a bone.

Our flight with Taca Airlines departed and we soon touched down in San Jose. We were in transit and not allowed to disembark so we couldn't kiss the dirt in Costa Rica. But the pilots, Captain Fidel Melara and Rafael Cornejo, signed the log book to register our presence in the country. Fidel knew New Zealand well. Two years go he'd flown for Freedom Air and had been based in Hamilton. 'I loved every minute of it,' he said.

We arrived in San Salvador, the capital of El Salvador. A new motorway leads into the city, cutting through a landscaped green-belt. This was constructed after a monster earthquake two

Captain Fidel
Melara,
'Captain' James,
and co-pilot
Rafael Cornejo.

years earlier, which had wreaked havoc in the city. El Salvador is a very shaky country. Not only is it in a vigorous seismic zone, it has 20 volcanoes in its very small area.

We had to spend most of the day dashing from one airline office to the next to collect 12 new tickets and so we only snatched a look at San Salvador. It looks thoroughly Americanised with buildings spread through parks and trees. Although there were many armed paramilitary in dark fatigues, there was little sign of the civil war that raged here between 1979 and 1991 when 75,000 people were killed. The mood of the place seemed relaxed and amiable and we were sorry to be leaving so quickly.

One incident particularly warmed us to the place. Once again I left my now infamous painting behind, this time in a taxi I'd taken from the hotel into the town. Before I even registered its loss, the taxi driver drove back to the hotel and returned it.

28 Guatemala

Rescheduling meant we had to fly into Guatemala and out again on the same day. We had time to drive into the city's centre in a taxi bedecked with CD packets, plaster butterflies and tigers, and a collection of coins stuck to the glove box. There were some grand old buildings but many others that were run-down and unadorned. The gleaming guns of the guards who stood outside any building of note were often in better condition than the buildings they protected.

The city is land-locked and surrounded by wooded hills. People in bedraggled clothing walked aimlessly down the street, grimy kids loitering in their bare feet. Guatemala has a history of coups, dictatorships and guerrilla fighting, and a profound division persists between the Amerindian majority and the elite Latinos of mixed Spanish/Amerindian ancestry.

As we entered the airport terminal again we were surrounded by a gaggle of shoeshine boys in overworked clothing. They had no shoes themselves. I took a photograph of Elia Jose, an Amerindian boy of about eight who was small and skinny for his age. His teeth were stained and his face and hands streaked with dirt.

With the taxi driver as interpreter, I asked Jose what his dream was. He stared at me, incredulous. 'What is the point of that?' he said.

I tried again. 'If you could have anything you wanted, what would you choose?'

He shrugged. 'I would choose not to go to jail.'

Jail, we were told by our driver/interpreter, is not the worst thing that can happen to street kids in Guatemala.

As we made our way through Customs I noticed a poster of a handgun with a large red cross through it. Underneath it stood a real-life guard holding an enormous automatic rifle.

29 Mexico

The return flight to San Salvador from Guatemala was only 42 minutes, and after a three-hour transit we were on our way to Mexico. It was a crystalline night as we flew into Mexico City, the second largest metropolis in the world, and its lights stretched to the horizon on either side of us. Even the airport is the size of a small city. The distance from the arrival gate to the immigration area was about a kilometre and we were swept along it in a jostling eddy of humanity.

Our hotel, thank goodness, was only a 100-metre walk away from the terminal, connected to it by a bridge. It was an hour before midnight and we were not in a frame of mind to tackle Mexico City's polluted, overcrowded roads.

The size of the airport meant that James got a little of the exercise he yearned for, which had been difficult during the last week. I, on the other hand, was maintaining my normal regime, which mostly comprised walking to the smoking lounge at every airport. We'd had a lot of very early starts and late nights in the last few days and it was sleep, not exercise, which I craved.

Today, I reflected, we'd had breakfast in El Salvador, lunch in Guatemala, afternoon tea back in El Salvador and a very late dinner in Mexico. Now that's travelling.

30 Cuba

After intensive electronic and physical security scanning we boarded the Mexican Airlines flight bound for Havana. Several young Americans were flying with us. Mexico City is a popular departing point for Americans flying to Cuba, which has been out of bounds to them for the last 40 years. Despite the threat of imprisonment or hefty fines, 200,000 Americans visited Cuba in 2001 and found it affordable, interesting and, contrary to the US government's rhetoric, free of menace.

We left at the civilised hour of 10.15 a.m. but through lack of sleep we were still operating on autopilot. Isadore's potent tail continued to sting and we had to take a more southerly flight path than normal, which added some 640 kilometres to the journey but made for a remarkably smooth flight.

The landing in the difficult conditions was perfect. We were still on the plane when the pilot came out of the cockpit. Captain Rocio Rodriguez was a young, spectacularly attractive Mexican woman who, with long chestnut hair cascading from under her captain's cap, looked more like a model. She signed the record book for us and posed for a photograph.

All we needed to do in Havana was to enter the country to get a passport stamp and exit again. But the queue at immigration was long and didn't seem to be moving. We waited, first fretting and then fuming. When our flight departure was only about 20 minutes away from leaving we decided to abandon the stamp idea and peeled off to go back to the plane. It seemed a simple enough plan. And then a gang of armed security guards descended on us and, with much arm-waving and incomprehensible shouting, indicated that we must return to the queue.

We pleaded; then, in a growing crescendo of panic, we shouted. One officer spoke a little English and he listened, frowning with concentration. He translated what he'd understood to the small army that now surrounded us. They went into a huddle: more burbling and hand-waving. The officer reported back to us in very broken English: 'We do not believe you,' he said, glaring suspiciously.

We pulled out our itinerary, a six-inch wad of tickets and the record book, pointed to the logos on our shirts, and showed them our pre-issued return boarding passes. It was a waste of time. They had made up their minds that a couple of out-of-shape, badly-dressed chaps arriving from Mexico were up to no good.

James kept calm and tried to mime our requirements. I stormed back to the immigration area to join a now shorter line. Five minutes later I finally arrived in front of an immigration officer, who examined and re-examined every inch of my passport and then raised his stamp and poised it over the page.

There was an anguished bellow from one of the army contingent who ran towards us yelling, 'No stamp, no stamp.' He grabbed me by the arms and marshalled me into a nearby lift. A bewildered James was already there. This was getting serious. We'd worried that we might end up on the wrong side of some arcane law, but never thought it would be in Cuba.

Then the lift doors opened to a familiar view – the corridor to our departure gate. Our stay in Cuba was over. It transpired that Captain Rodriguez had worried when we hadn't turned up to reboard and had dispatched runners to find us.

Just over three hours later, and only seven hours after we had first left it, we were back at Mexico Airport. We decided to walk the kilometre to our hotel and then have a beer, which we felt had been well-earned.

We fell into the bar. 'Dos cervesas, por favor.' I congratulated myself on my expanding Spanish vocabulary. The waiter replied, 'No senor, no beer. Dry day in Mexico.'

This astonishing announcement turned out to be quite true. The citizens of Mexico City were voting on the construction of a controversial motorway and in an extraordinary manoeuvre the government had decreed that if they really wanted to force the issue to vote, then they would do it sober. We celebrated our return to Mexico with a can of Coke.

31 Honduras

The approach into the capital of Tegucigalpa (Tegus for short) revealed disintegrating roads lined by dilapidated, overcrowded shanties. We weren't staying long. A taxi took us to the Clarion Hotel to use its business facilities and there was just time for a quick trip to the centre of town. It was a noisy, polluted, frantic place situated in a dish-shaped valley ringed by mountains which were covered in pine trees.

Throughout the trip Avideo, the taxi driver, railed against the Catholic Church, which he blamed for too many children being born to families who could barely feed them. 'I have five children also,' he said, 'but for me it's okay.'

The Parque Central is, as its name suggests, the focus of the city. It fills an area in front of a magnificent 18th-century cathedral, which houses a great art collection that we didn't have time to see. The square was choked with vendors, strollers, police and street kids. We took a photograph for the children's book of a group of seven children playing around the central statue. They all came from the same family and there were even more at home.

'Children like these live on the streets and don't go to school,' said Avideo. 'And there is no point in giving their mothers money to help raise them. They (the mothers) just beg all day and fuck all night.'

Avideo lost his home in Hurricane Michelle which decimated Honduras in 1998, but he said he didn't want to beg and so he worked as hard as he could and now was able to rent a house for his family.

Honduras was once part of the great Mayan Empire which spanned Southern Mexico, Belize, Guatemala and El Salvador. In 2001, the eighth of the 16 surviving tombs of the Mayan rulers had been uncovered not too far from the city.

In a local paper James read that 53 children and youths had been murdered between 21 August and 21 September, which brought the total killed since 1998 to 1346. Honduras is a major transit point for the movement of cocaine from Colombia to Mexico and North America, and that does nothing to help its reputation for being the most violent city in Latin America. Gangs of youths, identified by tattoos of satanic emblems, roam the streets creating terror. Heavily-armed security forces were everywhere, supposedly to protect the public against bandits, robbers, murderers and drug dealers. 'We can't always trust the police either,' said Avideo.

32 Nicaragua

Managua, the capital of Nicaragua, has an up-to-date, air-conditioned airport. The end of the line of incoming passengers, kept orderly by means of ropes, reached the bottom of an escalator that fed into the arrivals hall. We were met with the sight of an escalator full of people walking backwards in an effort to stand still. Then an elderly woman gave up the struggle and allowed herself to be propelled forward, which caused a domino effect that shattered any attempt at order and caused a degree of panic. It was late at night and we were delighted to find that our hotel – the Camino Real – was only minutes from the airport. We collapsed into bed.

The next day our wake-up call ordered for 5 a.m. came at 5.45 a.m., just after we were startled awake by gunshots outside our window. To say that we prepared to depart quickly is an understatement. We literally threw our gear in the bags and ran out the door. In the foyer all was calm.

'Gunfire? Oh, that's just the skeet shooting,' the receptionist said.

The queue at the airport was so slow we wondered why we'd bothered to arrive on time. But the bonus was meeting Ninoska Garcia Paz, a plump woman whose beauty was not confined to her auburn hair. She was travelling to El Salvador to promote tourism to Nicaragua.

'Nicaragua has 45,000 "tourists" a year,' she told us. 'But that's not enough – 35,000 of them are US-based Nicaraguans returning to visit family. We grow coffee beans for export but at the moment it sells for 30 percent less than it costs to produce.'

'Why do they sell it at all?'

She shrugged. 'Our country is beautiful but poor, and unemployment is very high. In the past we have not been much better off than Haiti but things are improving. You must come back some time. Here in Managua you're in the west of the country where the Spanish settled. The English settled on the eastern Mosquito Coast. Managua's surrounded by lagoons which were the city's playground once but now they are in dismal shape ecologically.' Her enthusiasm rather outweighed the content of her sales pitch.

Another local woman waiting in the queue chimed into the conversation. 'They are,' she grumbled. 'On Tiscapa Lagoon the government built a floating amphitheatre but it sank and the seats were stolen and trees stripped for firewood. Hopeless!'

She looked a bit hopeless herself. She was thin and distraught-looking and weighed down with too much luggage. Strands of greasy hair had escaped her bun and were falling over her face in black streaks. We hadn't shaved for two days and we didn't look much better.

33 Belize

Belize was the last country we visited in Central America before we flew to New York for a few days' break. It also gave us the first really fine day we'd had since we left New Zealand.

On the flight in we'd met Andy Lee, a thickset Chinese man from Hong Kong who wore a slicked-back Elvis Presley hair-style. He lived with his family in the town of Benque. In this country of generous people, Andy stood out. He insisted on driving us into Belize City in his ageing Toyota Corolla and on the way he took on the role of a one-man Belize promotion board. By the time he pulled up outside the Princes San Egriso hotel, we wished we could have stayed much longer in Belize than the planned five hours.

Andy was the owner of a hotel in Benque, a town near the border with Guatemala, and he was met by the Princes Hotel's Turkish vice-president, Hamdi Karagozaglu, who insisted we have lunch on him. 'It is the best buffet in Belize,' said Andy loyally.

Belize, formerly British Honduras, is unlike its more volatile Central American neighbours in that it has never had a coup. 'It's a quiet, laid-back place,' Andy said. Hamdi nodded in agreement.

'Street crime is on the rise in the city but the countryside is mountainous and wild,' said Hamdi. 'We grow a lot of sugar but half the land is still covered in dense jungle, and there are many sanctuaries. You can see jaguars, anteaters, armadillos, pumas, ocelots, tapirs, toucans, macaws, crocodiles, boa constrictors and plenty of Mayan ruins.' He ticked off this wildlife on his fingers.

The Caribbean sea coast, washed by clear blue water, has some of the best diving areas in the world and a coral reef only second in size to Australia's.

After lunch we had work to do in the hotel's business centre. There we met Dave Meyers, a sallow-skinned lay preacher from a Catholic mission at Bengu Biejo del Carmen, who was killing time between dropping off nuns at the airport and picking up some more. Dave was from Virginia and prior to the clocks clicking over to 01.01.2000 based on his conviction that the US banking system was about to collapse, he had sold up everything he owned and invested in gold. Unkempt in sandals and a loose T-shirt, he looked like an ageing, rather agitated hippy. He was going to the airport, he said, and would we like a ride?

On the way we toured through the old town in his bright red ute. The centre of Belize was a crush of people with pavements shimmering under the heat, a ramshackle place of unpainted, wooden, British Caribbean-style buildings and open canals running in from the sea. Houses on stilts were crammed along their banks and moored in the water were lines of scruffy commuter dinghies.

At one point Dave stopped to collect supplies for the mission. On the other side of the road was an old wooden pole-house with a group of children playing in the dirt beneath it. Their mother sat on the rickety steps with a baby in her lap. I sauntered over to take a photograph and discovered that they were the family of the former superintendent of police. I photographed his six-year-old son, a small skinny lad in a grubby singlet with a noticeable scar on his chest. His name was Brendon Jeffries. 'I dream that my Papa come home,' he said.

By way of explanation his mother grimaced and said, 'One man cannot have two women!'

On the way to the airport we passed a cemetery. I expressed interest and in doing so caused our first near-death experience since we'd left South America.

Dave decided to give me a closer view and executed a U-turn in front of a fast-moving oncoming truck. We very nearly visited the cemetery permanently. I grabbed the steering wheel and by some miracle impact was avoided.

James was in the back of the ute trying to focus the video camera on the impending collision—a record of our last moments to be recovered by loved ones. 'The only thing I could see in the lens,' he said later, 'was my own life flashing before me.'

Both vehicles came to rest slewed across the road snugly side-by-side like nuzzling lovers. There was, however, no love between the drivers. Much loud, eye-to-eye Belizian dialogue took place before the other man continued on his way. Dave closed his eyes and muttered up a prayer of thanks. Inwardly I did the same.

A prayer was, perhaps, a fitting gesture for our last moments of the Latin American part of the journey. James and I were both sorry to be leaving. Mixed in with all the poverty and mayhem was a kind of vivid exuberance that we would miss.

34 United States of America

On 24 September, 28 days after we had left Auckland, we flew to New York via San Salvador, our sixth transit through that airport in the last few days, to spend four catch-up days with our wives. Anna flew in from New Zealand and Nicola from Brisbane, and we spent the time relaxing, checking gear, making onward arrangements and writing up diaries and logs.

Staying in one place for a few days felt like treading water after the speed of the last few weeks.

Looking back on the first month it all seemed amazingly straightforward. We were handling the flying and despite dodgy destinations, very little sleep and a hectic regime, neither of us were sickening. James and I were relatively at ease with each other: we shared a similar sense of humour which helped.

There were irritants, of course. James had to get used to my inability to relax. I didn't sleep much and whenever I was awake I had to be doing something. He was more contemplative, and needed to wind down from time to time. He dealt with my snoring (of which he had been warned) by playing music through headphones on his mini-disc player and sleeping like a baby to the strains of *On the Beach* and *The Art of Tea*.

The thing that was incredibly frustrating was our inability to get onto I-Pass, Telecom's worldwide Internet connection system. (Later we discovered that our account had simply not been activated by Telecom.) This meant that wherever we were, we had to chase around finding high-speed Internet connections for sending reports and making forward bookings, and it drove us crazy.

35 Canada

On the last day of September we were to fly to Toronto. Feeling fresh and ready to start the next phase of our travels we took the subway to La Guardia Airport. Air Canada had just been voted Best Airline for 2002, and so we were in a confident frame of mind. Bad idea. Not only had our booked flight to Toronto been oversold, but so had the next one that left an hour later. Our unlovely display of pouting and pleading worked, because in 10 minutes we were handed our boarding tickets.

'I managed to find two seats on the first flight,' said the supervisor, looking pleased with herself. 'Just hand these to that woman over there.' She pointed to another supervisor. But supervisor Mark II looked at the passes with a perplexed frown. 'I'm real sorry,' she said. 'These seat are for row 29. There are only 27 rows on this plane. Please stand over there.'

Standing 'over there' we noticed that an Air Canada flight to Ottawa was boarding at the next gate. We enquired and found that seats were available. We exchanged boarding passes and made for the aircraft, leaving behind some rather flustered Air Canada ground staff. Instant plan changes are possible when you don't have checked-in luggage.

In Ottawa we stayed in the Hotel Chima whose manager was a long-time friend of mine, Kevin Kluts. We dragged the rain with us to Ottawa, as we had through all the Americas. A quick tour of the city next day was watered down by heavy showers and a cold wind. It was still a beautiful city, spreading out from the south bank of the Ottawa River. The air was clean, the streets wide and the parks extensive, and there was some sensational architecture: the elegant spires, turrets, stonework and statues of the old, mixed in with towering, modern high-rise buildings of glass and steel. As Canada's capital, the city was dominated by large and handsome Parliament buildings.

Dave, our taxi driver, was an Afghan who on his left cheek sported a puckered scar from a gunshot wound. He showed us another on his wrist. Both were inflicted by Russian sub-machine-gun bullets. 'Under my shirt there are two more,' he said. 'My shoulder still has a bullet embedded in it and it aches in the cold.' Dave had fought in Afghanistan during what he called 'the civil wars', but he would not tell us who he was fighting for. 'It was a crappy group,' he said. 'I was there for the excitement and too young to know what I was doing.'

Despite these scars of combat, Dave reckoned that the Uzbekistan/Afghanistan border, which we would soon be crossing, was relatively safe. And he told us how to handle Afghanistan's complex political problems. It was stunning in its simplicity: 'Live somewhere else,' he said.

The next day we flew back to the US. At Boston Airport, 35 days and 35 nations into the All Nations Quest, we boarded a flight to Dublin and the European leg of the journey.

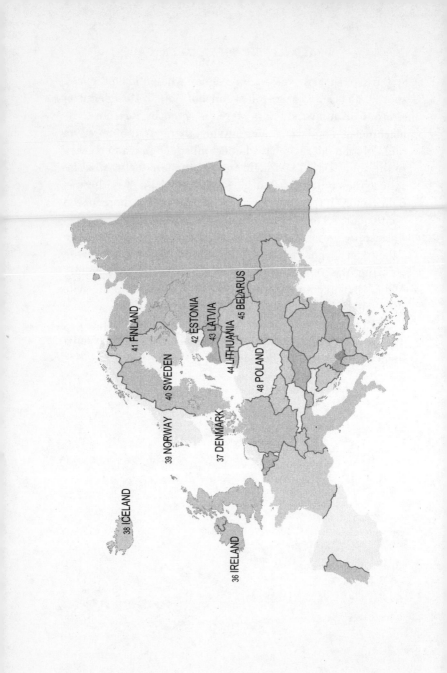

36 IRELAND
38 ICELAND
39 NORWAY
37 DENMARK
40 SWEDEN
41 FINLAND
42 ESTONIA
43 LATVIA
44 LITHUANIA
45 BELARUS
48 POLAND

CHAPTER SIX

Ireland and Scandinavia

36 Ireland

The five-hour flight to Shannon was filled with Irish charm. We didn't sleep and felt decidedly sluggish by the time we landed in the Emerald Isles where, of course, it was raining.

We drank an Irish coffee to fill in the time before we left for Dublin. On the wall behind the bar was the portrait of Joe Sheridan, the drink's inventor: when flying-boat passengers arrived here they were, like us, cold and exhausted, so Joe would add a tot of whiskey to their coffee to perk them up.

We saw nothing of Ireland as we flew north. We were still towing wet weather. Grey Ireland merged with a rag-grey sky.

At Dublin we hired a car to take us to Drogheda, about 40 kilometres to the north, where we were being interviewed by a local radio and newspaper.

'This is our 36th day on the move,' I was able to tell them. 'And Ireland is the 36th nation we've visited. We've travelled 47,626 kilometres, on 50 flights and 20 different airlines, and stayed in 33 hotels.' Our interviewers looked suitably impressed, and for the first time in all of our interviews didn't ask why we were doing the Quest. For that alone, we loved the Irish.

We sleep-walked through the rest of the day and half-way through the afternoon dragged ourselves back to Dublin Airport, where we sat like stunned mullets waiting for our evening flight to Copenhagen.

It had been a big 24 hours.

37 Denmark

Our time in Copenhagen was brief. We arrived at 9 p.m. and just under 12 hours later left for the airport again, so the only thing I can say about the city is that it has a spectacular airport with an impressive line-up of restaurants and retail shops glittering with product.

I was surprised that we couldn't use Euros and said so to the clerk at the SAS service desk. She drew herself up and said primly, 'We do not have the Euro. We love our King and Queen and do not wish to take their faces off our banknotes.'

A new, smooth, fast and punctual train took us to Central Station, which was a stone's throw from Mercure Copenhagen where we stayed. In the bar that night we heard that another hurricane had ripped through the Yucatán where 95,000 homes had already been destroyed by Hurricane Isadore. People died on St Vincent and in Jamaica, and St Lucia lost half its banana crop. In the cool sophisticated milieu of Copenhagen it seemed a long way away.

38 Iceland

We flew down through the cloud which hung about Keflavik Airport and saw below a flat and featureless land. The airport was built by the Americans in 1941 as a staging post for the Allies and was now the commercial airport as well as a US military base.

For the second time on the Quest our camera decided to take a journey on its own when we left it in the taxi after the 40-kilometre journey into Reykjavik. It was returned within the hour. Desparation being the mother of invention forced me there and then to work out a way to clip it to my pack so it wouldn't happen again.

Reykjavik is in the flat swampy southwest of the island. It is the world's most northern capital, and all heating is provided geothermally. The island has long enjoyed peace, a good standard of living and a stable economy, and the only real health risk is hypothermia.

In the lounge of the Keflavik Hotel we met Thrainn. He had been drinking with a friend at another table but when his companion left he came over to us, sat down heavily in an empty chair and ordered another Jagermeister (schnapps). He'd evidently already had quite a few.

He was an Icelander but unlike his Viking ancestors he was tall and dark. 'You're from New Zealand?' he asked, eyeing our shirts. 'The home of Peter Blake. I know him. I am a very keen sailor. In fact I'm a fokkin keen sailor.'

Thrainn was a pilot with Iceland Air. 'Man, I just fokkin love it up there,' he said, rolling his eyes extravagantly towards the ceiling. 'Most people here earn their living from fishing, so it's easy to be a fokkin keen sailor. But me, I just fokkin love flying.'

Thrainn insisted that we join him for dinner but as time wore on and one Jagermeister followed another, the chances of his being a coherent dinner companion receded. We excused ourselves and fled. I hoped he wasn't going to be our pilot next day.

Thrainnless, we later dined on at a local restaurant (which was full of Americans from the air base — Iceland hibernates in winter and tourists stay away) on pan-fried skotuselur, a delightfully tasty and textured fish. Some very strange dishes have been developed in Iceland: we might have been offered hakarl, shark meat buried up to six months to add flavour; whale meat; seal meat; roast puffin; hrutspungur, pickled rams' testicles; or svie, a whole boiled sheep's head.

39 Norway

Iceland Air flew us to Oslo. When we arrived we were phoned by Philip Crabtree, director of Save the Children (Norway). He was incredulous that we had arrived from Iceland. 'I thought you were biking around the world,' he said.

Oslo was an expensive but wonderful place with a laid-back, almost rural atmosphere. Philip introduced us to the office staff and then took us around this oldest of the Scandinavian capitals. In the small central city are theatres, galleries and museums, including the Edvard Munch Museum dedicated to Norway's most famous painter. Philip steered us to the vast Vigeland Park where we meandered along wide avenues past life-sized statues which the celebrated Gustave Vigeland had sculpted in a great variety of poses. The trees were on fire with the colours of autumn. The wind pushed fallen leaves around our feet and watery sunlight occasionally filtered down from a covering of heavy cloud. The temperature had plummeted: for the first time we needed our Icebreaker merino-wool jerseys.

Most of our evening was taken up chasing elusive visas and rearranging our itinerary. Shifts in scheduling and world events meant that changing our bookings was a never-ending process.

Everything was so alarmingly expensive that we were almost too scared to go out. In the hotel café, a small hamburger and fries and a lemonade cost $NZ60. James moaned about the price to a Norwegian at the next table who smiled indulgently and said, 'That's nothing to us. We are so well-off it is almost embarrassing. North Sea oil and good management means we have no foreign debt and almost no unemployment.'

Early next day on a still, dark and chilly morning, we 'floated' out to the airport on a very modern train. On the television in a corner of the carriage we watched headline news and the latest stockmarket reports as we passed through wooded hills dripping with autumn colours.

 40 Sweden

We continued to drag bad weather with us. In Stockholm we brought the first snow of winter to Sweden, turning the city wet and chillingly cold.

We took a canal tour and then a walk around Gamla Stan (old town) with a thousand other tourists who choked the narrow, cobblestone streets. Stockholm is a dramatically beautiful city that covers 14 islands linked by 53 bridges. It's racier than the other Scandinavian capitals, with a harder commercial edge. James, who was keeping up his walking regime mainly to keep warm, was astonished by the young women walking around the streets hunched in jackets and scarves and woolly hats but with exposed midriffs showing off their navel rings.

The best way to get around Stockholm was on the T, the clean and very efficient underground system that radiates out from T-Centralen, a massive station carved from rock, the rough walls painted in vivid murals. But we went by ferry to Vasamuseet, a museum which demonstrated 17th-century life at sea. Housed in the building was Sweden's largest-ever wooden galleon,

Save the Children Office - Oslo.

the *Vasa*. It was to be the pride of the king's fleet, but it was so unwieldy that as it was launched in Stockholm's harbour it capsized and ignominiously sank, in full view of the king, where it remained until it was salvaged in 1962.

The next morning we went to collect visas from the Belarusian consulate which was on another island; we bought cheap gloves and hats to help us rug up for the cold outdoor climate; and dickered around with arrangements for the onward journey. Among the many headaches were the Uzbekistan visas. Double-entry visas had arrived from London but we needed four. Libya was still refusing any visas at all.

The final ride to the Stockholm Airport was with Mario, an Iranian, who had his own visa problems. Swedish authorities were balking at issuing a visitor permit for his Russian mother. We knew how he felt.

It was dusk when we flew on a Finnair MD82 over a soggy landscape pocked with numerous lakes and ploughed fields glowing white with frost.

41 Finland

Helsinki was smaller and more intimate than Scandinavia's other capitals, but the many Russian-influenced buildings clustered around the harbour gave it a more pragmatic, provincial look. The hub was a waterside square and fish market surrounded by functional 19th-century buildings and colourful wooden fishing boats moored in the viaduct.

On the way to the airport next morning we stopped at the square to look at the annual herring market. Following a 200-year tradition, herring and fish products are sold in canvas stalls from an impressive line-up of containers.

We left Scandinavia with a mixture of trepidation and excitement. Ahead of us was five days and sleepless nights travelling though Estonia, Latvia, Lithuania, Belarus, Moscow, Ukraine, Slovakia, Hungary, Moldova and Bucharest. Something was bound to go wrong.

CHAPTER SEVEN

THE BALTICS

42 Estonia

It was snowing steadily as we waited at Oslo airport for the flight to Tallinn in Estonia. We shivered and cast envious glances at an over-sized black fur hat worn by a tall, self-assured man on the other side of the departure lounge.

He saw our glances and came over. 'I am Peter,' he said. 'I have watched you looking at my hat. You must get one. I was sitting at an airport today, resting the hat on my knee when a small boy came up and asked if he could stroke the cat. I told him: "No, no, this is not a cat," and put it on my head to show him. The little fellow burst into tears. "You should not put a cat on your head,"' he said.

Peter Woolsey, a willowy Englishman in his early 60s, lived half of each week in Tallinn and the rest in various cities around

Europe. He invited us to dinner that evening and when we arrived in Tallinn insisted on driving us through the old town. We were enchanted with the hodgepodge of medieval walls, spires, turrets and weaving cobbled streets. After Scandinavia they were pleasantly devoid of tourists. We also passed a burgeoning new business sector setting up in converted historical buildings – an indication, I thought, of the brave, optimistic spirit that has never left these patriotic people.

The Balts' struggle for nationhood culminated when two million Estonians, Latvians and Lithuanians formed a human chain stretching from Tallinn in the north to Vilnius in the south and called for secession. And so after years of Soviet occupation with its murders, purges and deportations, the Baltic States finally won their independence in 1991. There was nothing desolate about the people we met in the Baltics. They were extraordinarily attractive, especially the women who were fresh-skinned and vital and full of shining smiles. The years of oppression were worn lightly by the younger generation.

We stayed that night in a converted monastry called the Domina Ilmarina and dined with Peter in an old, dimly lit Italian restaurant called Contra Vino. Peter's partner Svetlana came with us. She was a strikingly beautiful 23-year-old Russian, tall and slim with long fair hair and large blue eyes. Over pasta and red wine Peter told us how when she was 13 and the Russians occupied Estonia, she had been a promising gymnast. After independence all opportunities were denied her and she hadn't enough money to go back to Russia. 'I am trying to help her,' he said.

'And who could blame you, mate,' James muttered, with a glance at Svetlana's stunning profile.

We finished the meal with a glass of very fine grappa and then James walked with Svetlana and Peter to the Hollywood Club a few streets away. The walk through those ancient streets with a light drizzle furring the arcs of orange street lighting was more memorable than the club. 'As we walked into the club,' James said later, Peter whispered conspiratorially, "Svetlana is mine. But you can have any other girl you fancy."' It was a nice thought. The girls of the Baltic States were probably the most beautiful in the world and the room was full of them. James hastily pointed out that he is a very happily married man.

43 Latvia

In the six hours we had in Riga, Latvia's capital, we were blessed with sunshine, and not so blessed with a temperature of four degrees Centigrade. The old city's narrow lanes and streets lead past old two-storeyed, pastel-coloured buildings to various squares, each dominated by a church or government building. Our hotel was on the river opposite the palace of the president, currently a Canadian Latvian woman, Varia Vike-Freiberga, who was elected in 1999.

We spent two hours in the Occupation Museum, a huge concrete building raised on pillars, where exhibits were devoted to the period of Russian occupation after World War II when one third of the country's population was murdered. Many Russians still lived in Latvia. They had come for work after the war, through a scheme called the 'Economic Investment by the Brotherly Republic', and never went back. Understandably they were now treated as second-class citizens and had limited opportunities.

44 Lithuania

Lithuania is similar to the two other Baltic nations but much smaller. We arrived in Vilnius, the capital, at around 7.30 p.m., then walked through the old town's charming narrow streets past a plethora of hidden courtyards, cafés, bars and nightclubs and ate at a café opposite the Concert Hall.

Vilnius was once a very important Jewish city and the Jewish ghetto still stands, but the new, unadorned, Russian-influenced architecture has added little of character.

Late the next morning we boarded an old Passat bus to take us to Minsk in Belarus where, that night, we had to be at the airport in time to catch a plane to Moscow. It was in the countryside that the legacy of a tough history was evident. Very few of the technological advances found in Vilnius existed in the towns and farms that we passed. The starkness of the flat land was relieved only by a scattering of wooden houses tucked in behind clumps of autumn-leafed trees, and small pockets of habitation hunkered in the valleys. Most transport was in primitive horse-drawn carts. The road was wide but in poor condition and our own progress was so slow at times that we could have been overtaken by a horse.

The further east we travelled the more primitive things became. In the fields ploughmen walked behind single discs pulled by a horse: the turned soil looked overworked and infertile. Farmers sowed their fields by scattering handfuls of seed from baskets slung around their necks.

We saw only one tractor on the journey to Minsk and, according to Danny, it would have been community-shared. Danny Shinkevich was a 21-year-old Belarusian, short of stature and short of hair. A gregarious character, a kind of Jack-the-lad wide-boy, he was returning to Belarus from a four-month stay with his girlfriend in the US. As many young Balts do, he spoke very passable English.

Leaving Lithuania and passing into Soviet-influenced Belarus took about the same length of time it had taken us to bus to the border. We had to endure two hours of official paper-shuffling before we were allowed through. As we approached Belarusian Customs, Danny's ebullient sense of humour faded and was replaced by finger-chewing agitation. He had a criminal conviction, he explained, and was seriously worried about what might happen to him if it became known.

Border guards in green tunics stepped into the bus and glowered at us. Danny, sabotaged by his nerves, made some inane remark and giggled. He was the only passenger hauled off the bus.

About 10 minutes later he returned full of bravado. 'They only searched my luggage,' he said. 'They found nothing.' And when the bus had crossed the border he stood up and brazenly tore his Customs document in two. 'They can't get me now,' he said.

A minute later the bus jerked to a stop and the door opened. Danny blanched. Three menacing-looking men with hands as broad as spades climbed aboard and lumbered to take up seats at the back of the bus. Danny recovered his composure.

45 Belarus

Across the border fences disappeared and most animals, except the ubiquitous flocks of geese, were tethered. Under a blank grey sky the countryside looked forlorn and abandoned. Belarus is a flat boggy bit of land between Poland and Russia. Its highest peak, Mt Dzyarzhynskaya, is only 346 metres. It was also devastated by a succession of foreign powers, and ravaged by both World Wars. The German invasion in 1941 saw the deaths of 1.3 million people and the virtual annihilation of the country's Jewish population.

Our only stop on the way was at a rough little village called Oshmyany. Years of neglect were evident. The public buildings were falling apart and the roads were pocked with muddy potholes. There was snow on the ground and people at the bus stop were pacing around breathing into their hands and trying to keep warm. It looked like a scene from the movie, *Dr Zhivago*.

Calm after the bother — Danny Shinkevich relaxes after
crossing the Belarus border.

Through Danny I asked an old peasant if I could take her
photo. Her head was wrapped in a typical gold-and-yellow scarf.
Her face, sans teeth, was as crumpled and white as freshly
kneaded dough. In answer she hurled Belarusian abuse at
Danny, who summarised its content. 'She says, don't fuck with
my head!'

We took a photo instead of a statue of Lenin which we were
surprised to see was still standing. According to Danny, no one
gets too uptight about Lenin effigies any more. 'It's just history,'
he said. 'There are storage rooms where all the statues of Lenin
and Stalin have been thrown because nobody quite knows what
to do with them.'

On the outskirts of Minsk we saw a new suburb being built. It
was awful. Just rows of simple stacked apartment blocks with
nothing to relieve the repetition. We joined a stream of Ladas,
trolleys and tractors making for the city centre. Hitch-hikers
from all walks of life, including policemen, thumbed the

vehicles down. Everywhere we looked tall chimneys were belching smoke into the heavy air.

When the Germans left the city in 1944 there was hardly a stone left standing. It had to be rebuilt, so there is a new-broom look about the place with an emphasis on utility rather than decoration. Both the river and the streets are wide and flat, the buildings and parks uniform and sterile. It was in this uninspiring environment that James and I first seriously thought it was all over.

At the bus stop Danny instructed a burly driver and his swarthy mate to take us straight to the airport. We climbed into the back of an unmarked and ancient VW Passat and waved goodbye to Danny, who looked rather uncertain. Neither man spoke English. For half an hour we drove along the freeway but there was no reassuring airport signage anywhere. Then suddenly our taxi turned off onto an unsealed and very narrow road which was closely hemmed in by woods. In my mind that was it. I could see the epitaph on my headstone: 'Robbed and murdered in Minsk.' For some reason we both felt strangely resigned to this fate. We looked at each other, opened our mouths to say something, shut them again and sped like lambs to the slaughter.

The taxi spun around another corner to the right and there in front of us was a high concrete wall topped with razor wire – the back end of the airport. Instead of cutting our lives short, our hulky friends – now our very good friends – had taken a short cut.

We screeched to a halt in the dilapidated taxi outside what we assumed was Minsk Airport. It was 5.30 p.m. and the huge terminal in front of us was devoid of life. Only 20 cars were parked in the enormous carpark. We entered the building. Still nobody. The lights were off. The temperature inside was the same as outside, so cold that we exhaled in misty puffs. We turned right and walked to the end of the building, and the only signs of life were a diminutive barman whose head just cleared

Minsk airport - and nothing happened.

the counter and three guards in army fatigues leaning on the bar huddled in a haze of cigarette smoke. No one looked up as we walked past.

At the end of the building we turned around and plodded back in the other direction and behind a glass wall found what appeared to be check-in counters. Again, no lights and no people. We trudged back to the bar because we didn't know what else to do. This time we had a nodding exchange with the guards. We ordered Bajithka, an excellent Russian beer at $US1 for a large bottle, and sipped our way through three glassfuls each while we waited for something to happen.

After an hour, an announcement echoed through the hall, first in Russian and then in Oxford English. Check-in was now open. We swallowed the last of the beer and made our way to the counter to line up with a handful of other passengers. Minsk is a city of some two million people, who were obviously out of pocket or not keen on flying: the only people in the departure lounge were a tired-looking mother in a furry coat trying to soothe her two small children, a bedraggled youth who looked as if he'd just come from the Afghan front, and a man in a shiny blue suit and slicked-back hair who looked like local mafia. The room itself was exceedingly stark, just a few chairs, and ashtrays everywhere – usually placed beneath the no smoking signs.

From the lounge we could see the Belavia Airlines Tupolev 134-3 that was about to give us our first experience on a Russian aircraft. The only plane on the runway, it was surrounded by ancient fuel and service trucks. It had strange wings that sloped downwards and looked as if they were going to drag along the ground. As we stood appraising it, we saw two wolves slink across the tarmac and disappear behind a group of World War II-style buildings.

At the call to board we felt our way down a dark unlit stairwell and out past the Tupolev's glassed-in nose, which reminded me of a Lancaster bomber. We deviated for a closer look at this peculiar feature and gave a cheery wave to the engineer in the cockpit. He waved back limply.

It was freezing – zero degrees Centigrade – and the wind tore viciously at any exposed skin. The queue of people boarding the plane was gathered in a frigid bunch at the base of the rickety stairs leading up to it, waiting for those who were already on board to stow their many possessions on the narrow overhead shelves. There were no lockers.

We were last on and had to keep our bags on our knees until a plump matronly-looking women in the row beside us indicated that we could put them on the vacant seat beside her. She then generously offered us a handful of chocolate-covered almonds. We grasped them gratefully. We'd been moving so fast that we hadn't eaten in the last 14 hours and the on-board dinner that followed was a surprisingly tasty ploughman's lunch served with a glass of Moldovan wine.

The inside of the Tupolev was not glamorous: the tray tables were made of thin metal and when everybody was eating the clattering sounded like a payout from a poker machine; old brown vinyl covered the walls and the seats were cramped. Incongruously beautiful hand-woven rugs covered the floor and despite its age, the Tupelov never gave us moment's anxiety as to its safety.

46 RUSSIA

47 UKRAINE
48 POLAND
49 CZECH REP
50 SLOVAKIA
51 HUNGARY
52 MOLDOVA
53 ROMANIA
54 TURKEY
58 KAZAKHSTAN
55 UZBEKISTAN
57 KYRGYZSTAN
56 TAJIKISTAN
60 TURKMENISTAN
59 AZERB.

CHAPTER EIGHT

Eastern Europe

46 Russia

The descent into Moscow was not accompanied by your usual messages from the crew, but seemed to be a catalyst for passengers to bring out their mobile phones and start making calls. I was still typing on my laptop as we landed! We peered through the large porthole windows and saw snow and the ground crew's smoking exhalations. The doors opened and we were hit by a chilly blast of air. Inside the terminal, an ill wind of a completely different nature was about to hit us.

Because we were intending merely to transit through Moscow, we had no Russian visas and so looked out for the Transit Lounge sign. We knew that there either wasn't one or that we had missed it when we found ourselves outside in the snow. There was nothing else to do but to check in at the Aerosvit

Russia – Tupolev at Minsk airport.

counter for our flight on to Kiev and confidently presented our tickets and boarding passes at immigration. Something was seriously wrong. Several officials went into a huddle and began a vigorous discussion. A podgy officious woman, with auburn hair and legs that could have kicked a rugby goal from half-way, stumped over to us.

'No transit visa, beeeg problem,' she said in a voice heavy with authority. 'Minsk–Moscow–Minsk, okay. Minsk–Moscow–Kiev, *nyet*. Beeeg problem.' She indicated that we should stand to one side of the desk. Twenty minutes later she indicated we should stand to the other side of the desk. An hour later we were unsmilingly ushered into an office at the back of the immigration hall and ordered to sign a piece of paper. It was in Russian.

The only English words we heard were 'beeeg problem' and 'protocol'. There was little point in asking if we were signing approval for our banishment to the Gulag Archipelago. Meanwhile, our booked flight to Kiev had already departed.

A guard motioned us to sit back in the departure hall. We made our way to the bar and ordered a beer. Time passed. We drank more beer. Two women in very short khaki immigration service skirts and high black boots, approached us as if they'd been assigned as our guards. They ordered a beer each, perched on the stools next to ours, raised their glasses and nodded at us in a companionable way. We nodded and smiled back. We drank more beer.

A third officer joined us, a slim severe-looking woman with the sort of spiked hair that makes you think of a pencil sharpener. She spoke a little English: 'You go to Russian consular, Terminal 2,' she said. After an exchange of charades we learned that this was to be found in a separate building.

It was now minus two degrees. The night was black but James was determined we should walk. We trudged through the residue of the last snowfall, which was the colour of soot. Then, after a kilometre when the bitter wind had almost frozen our cheeks and our trousers were splattered in slush, I lost confidence in our direction and turned back. Half-way along this retreat a bus going in the opposite direction drew up beside us. The doors opened and we climbed on board. By that stage we were so cold and the environment was so menacing that we didn't really care where it was going.

Fifteen minutes later, and about six kilometres away from Terminal 1, the bus stopped outside Terminal 2. Of course the consular office did not pop up in front of us. We walked around for about twenty minutes looking for it. By then, the cold, the exercise and the anxiety had dropped our blood-sugar levels and we stopped to buy an ice-cream. On the wall next to the vendor's stall was an intercom and under it was written in Russian and in a tiny English transcript: 'To contact the consular office, push the button and wait.'

We pushed and waited. *Nyet*. We tried again. Still nothing. Then the ice-cream vendor, a small bristly little woman in a huge white apron, walked over, grabbed the phone and bellowed a string of instructions or abuse into the mouthpiece. Within minutes Uri appeared – a most efficient-looking fellow in a light brown, tweed jacket. With his sharp features, neat goatee beard and debonair air he looked like a schoolteacher. His English was excellent. We described our situation.

'Ah, the problem,' he said, 'is that the flight from Minsk is treated as a domestic one and so technically you are in Russia without a visa. You must have an exit visa to get out again. There is, however, another problem. At one in the morning, that's in 20 minutes, the consulate will close and you do not have a ticket because the ones you have were for a flight that went yesterday. I cannot give you a transit visa without a valid ticket.'

'Give me 10 minutes,' James said. He pointed towards the Aeroflot counter. Uri nodded and said he'd be back. From the Aeroflot departure board we learned the number of a flight that was leaving later that morning and James wrote our own revalidation stickers. We had no idea where it was going or whether it had seats available.

Some 30 minutes later Uri reappeared carrying a wad of papers. He checked our revalidated tickets, gave a nod of approval and a wry smile, asked for our passports and $US300 cash and disappeared again. We waited another 30 minutes. The consulate office had closed 40 minutes ago. Then Uri reappeared and handed us a receipt and our passports in which was pasted an exit visa only. We were free to go.

All this beer-drinking and waiting had taken its toll. It was now 2 a.m. and we were done-in. We booked ourselves into the Airport Novotel and crashed onto the beds for five hours' kip.

Next morning back at the airport Aerosvit office, James removed the bogus revalidation stickers and rebooked flights to Kiev. And that was the end of the beeeg problem. One night in Moscow had cost us an arm and a leg.

When we were airborne we looked down to see the relationship of Terminal 1 to Terminal 2. There was none. They were at opposite ends of a very large airport. On the tarmac there was the amazing sight of hundreds of Russian aircraft lined up three to four deep for at least two kilometres. We sank back in the seats and visions of a sojourn in the Gulag faded with the view.

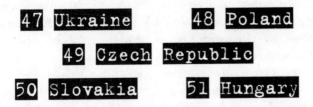

47 Ukraine   48 Poland
49 Czech Republic
50 Slovakia   51 Hungary

After a quick touch-down in Kiev in the Ukraine, we flew to Warsaw and had a cursory 'get our bearings for later' look around the grimy, stone-cold Warsaw Central Train Station which would once have been a very grand building.

There was time for only a quick flip around the old city. It was just a heap of rubble after World War II but there had been a huge reconstruction programme to restore its shattered ruins to a replica of the old city with bits of baroque, gothic and renaissance architecture. The Royal Way, which is the main drag, is a marvellous bit of road, lined with churches, palaces, galleries and museums.

Three hours later we boarded the Warsaw Express and located the three-square-metre cabin which was to be our home as we passed through the next four countries on our way to Budapest. Every bit of soft furnishing was bright red – the curtains, carpets, upholstery and cushions. James and I are both partially colour-blind, but unfortunately we can see red when it is the only colour.

Our guardian for the next 12 hours was a serious round-faced conductor called Wojaick. 'Yes, yes, I get you stamps everywhere we go,' he said, flushed with importance. He raised one bushy eyebrow as if to say 'these bastards are mad', but assured us he could also have the record book signed as we thundered through Poland, the Czech Republic, Slovakia and Hungary during the night. We still had to be woken up at each border crossing – eight times that night – but developed a system of opening the door and handing out our passports without leaving the bed covers.

Eventually a cold dawn light revealed rural Hungary before we slid into the industrial outskirts of Budapest and pulled to a stop at central station bang on time at 7.20 a.m. By then Wojaick was our best mate. He'd not only had our passports stamped but he'd methodically arranged for the record book to be witnessed. And we left his train with his stern paternal lecture ringing in our ears – a highly-coloured rundown on the unsavoury nature of every taxi driver in Budapest and the distinct possibility that we would be the victims of pick-pocket or mugger before the day was over. 'It is important you be very careful,' he said.

It was Sunday in Budapest and early risers were already about. Wojaick had so fired up our imaginations that they looked unkempt and brooding as if after a hard night out they were angling for a fight. We thought we'd keep a low profile. Couples were leaning groggily against each other on various park benches as we scuttled into the McDonald's next door to the railway station for coffee while we considered our next move.

We decided to ignore Wojaick's warning and flagged down a taxi to take us around the historic and stately centre of the city. The driver of the 15-year-old Mercedes, Jorge, seemed trust-worthy enough and conducted himself with an easy courtesy. He told us that things were heading in the right direction in Budapest, apart from the mafia-type gangs of Hungarians, Chinese, Turks and Russians that still fought for control of the city after dark. That happened mostly in the old city of Pest on the flat, east side of the river. On the hilly west side is the equally old city of Buda and the main residential area.

At a glance Budapest is stunningly beautiful with some incredible architecture. We drove over a number of the seven bridges that cross the blue Danube, which looked anything but blue that day. A grey Danube was unusual, because Budapest is one of the sunniest cities in Europe.

Later, at Ferihegy international airport, we bought tickets to Moldova for which we had no visas because not one Moldovan consulate anywhere had responded to our numerous entreaties by email, fax and phone calls. Without them we'd have to transit through the country, and fly straight to Romania, hoping that it was Moldova's loss rather than ours. As best as we could ascertain, the only export for the country was its wines: some of the best vines in Europe grew there. Andriss, the sales agent for Moldovan Airlines, contacted the ground staff at the airport in Chisinau to ensure that we would be met on arrival and helped to make a very quick transit so that we could carry on to Bucharest. Our experience in Russia had made us nervous.

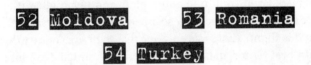

We bid Andriss goodbye and boarded a Saab 340 twin-prop aircraft. The cabin attendant single-handedly served up a hot meal and drinks to a full plane of over 30 passengers, a Herculean effort because onboard was a wrestling team from Hungary who demanded double helpings.

As we flew over northern Romania the skies cleared for about 15 minutes and we looked down on the Carpathian Mountains, the first high ground that we had seen since leaving Scandinavia. Then in Chisinau we were welcomed to Moldova by a smiling representative of Tarom Romanian Airlines. She gave us our onward boarding passes and told us that we were definitely missing something by not stopping. 'Moldova is very poor,' she said, 'but very pretty. The country's half-Russian and half-Romanian. There's been big trouble this year because the government tried to introduce Russian as the official language and most of us speak Romanian. Then the leader of the opposition disappeared under suspicious circumstances. Maybe it will be better when you come back.' She directed us to the transit lounge and within 20 minutes we had boarded the flight to Bucharest.

And there another 'beeeg' problem arose. We had changed our plans and forgotten that on the old schedule we were only going to transit through Romania. Once again we didn't have visas. It became clear, even though we grovelled and begged, that we were not going to enter that country without one. Our appearance didn't help. After two days on a train and two days of flying we were hardly looking our best.

We had two options: take a flight out that night to anywhere or spend the night on a bench in the transit lounge. We were exhausted and couldn't contemplate another night without a decent bed so we anxiously scanned the departure screen for a suitable flight. There was only one that went to a country that we hadn't yet visited and that was to Turkey. Damn the expense: we bought two new tickets to ensure our survival.

And so it came to pass that, a couple of hours later, looking as if we'd crossed into Turkey by camel we arrived in Istanbul. It was 10.30 p.m. and since we'd left Moscow the day before we'd travelled three air and five train sectors non-stop through eight countries. If this is a record, it comes under the heading of Stupidity.

Despite the hour and our failing physical condition, we negotiated a well-priced room in a hotel near the airport called the Florya Health Club. It seemed inapt that the owner/manager spent his waking hours sitting in the lobby chain-smoking.

But beds were all we required.

CHAPTER NINE

THE STANS

55 Uzbekistan

Things that start out badly don't necessarily end up that way. Our van to Istanbul airport to catch a flight to Tashkent in Uzbekistan was an hour late. The driver, a skinny man with one half-closed eye and a heavy moustache, stumbled through the side door to the hotel yabbering in Turkish: *'Cok uzuldum, cok uzuldum'* (sorry). He broke into English: 'The hotel – I couldn't find him. I no have map, nobody tell me where. *Cok uzuldum.'*

He also had an appalling sense of direction and with the aid of my tourist map I had to guide our guide to the airport, arriving minutes before the flight closed. The desk staff at Uzbekistan Airlines looked miffed that we had arrived at all. They had oversold the economy section and our no-show had solved their problem. Thanks to our tardy driver, we found ourselves upgraded to first-class where we had the luxury of leg-room.

The thought of flying on Uzbekistan Airlines had given me twinges of apprehension. But my fear was unfounded. The airline's main international routes were now serviced by brand-new Airbuses. The old Russian Tupolevs and Antonovs either had been mothballed or were being used for domestic flights.

On the ground in Tashkent, however, we were dogged by petty hassles and things fell apart. It took two hours to get bags from the plane to the conveyor belt, the wrong information was written on the flight board, and we were asked for money by an airport official for the heinous crime of being without a second Customs form, which nothing had indicated we needed. Access to cash by ATM was unavailable; credit cards were not accepted. In exchange for $US20, we received an inch-thick wad of local notes. Inflation was rampant in Uzbekistan. In the streets we saw people carrying plastic 'sacks' with handles, obviously off to purchase something major. You'd need a wheelbarrow of cash to buy a TV.

Apart from that, Tashkent was more modern and sophisticated than we had imagined but, built on flat land, was not particularly attractive. Evidence of the city's 2000-year history was mostly destroyed by an earthquake in 1966 and the town's centre was rebuilt by the Russians. In keeping with Soviet architectural style, it lacked personality. But from the window of the Sheraton Hotel we could see the elegant gold dome and minarets of a large mosque which must have survived the earthquake.

In the hotel bar that night we were entertained by a pianist who, in dark glasses and black fedora hat, looked like one of the Blues Brothers. Graceful belly-dancers gyrated enticingly, girls in halter-neck tops, fishnet stockings and hot pants minced around serving Kazakhstan beer. It all seemed risqué for a town that is 88 percent Muslim.

56 Tajikistan

We had ordered a taxi to drive south to the Tajikistan border the next morning. It was the first time we'd had to use unscheduled transport to get from one country to another.

Tajikistan lies between Uzbekistan, Afghanistan, China, Kyrgyzstan and Pakistan. The reason for its peculiar shape is that in 1929 Stalin ordered it to be carved out of Uzbekistan in an attempt to deal with Tajik resistance to the Soviet regime. The resentment continued and since the country's independence in 1991 ethnic hostility has led to hundreds being killed or fleeing. We were not particularly sorry that our visit was going to be brief.

We joggled our way to the nearest Tajikistan border crossing, close to Buston (pronounced Boston) 150 kilometres away, passing flat stretches of cotton and stubbly fields of hay both being harvested by hand. Much of it was being transported along the road tied to the roofs of small Ladas.

The road was also shared with horse-drawn carts piled dangerously high with produce. On the gravel verges small makeshift stalls sold anything from mobile telephone accessories to laundry detergent and fresh fruit. At one point we passed a huge bazaar held under rows of pergolas that had once been quite decent steel structures. Now tatty sacks and bits of plastic provided the only shelter.

Our driver was Bohodir Mirsamikov, a slender, self-assured man. Several times policemen waiting by their vehicles flagged him off the road and demanded money. Bohodir, his expression resigned, would smooth his oiled black hair off his face and pay up. Police were referred to as mafia because they were constantly finding ways to top up their meagre salary. They were despised, but at least they earned a living.

Tashkent was our hub for excursions into the other Stans but because we had been issued with only two entry permits into

Uzbekistan instead of four we had a problem. Because we merely had to walk across the 100-metre strip of no-man's-land into Tajikistan and then return, we mime-begged officials to let us re-enter Uzbekistan without using one of our precious visas. A pale young man in a very white shirt stepped forward and introduced himself: 'I am Iskandar Mirsaidov. I work here for the Swiss Peace Fund. Can I help?'

Speaking Russian, he explained the situation to the group of Uzbekistan police; but they were suddenly piously law-abiding. Fingering their AK47 guns and shaking their heads vigorously, they took our passports and stamped our exit.

We walked the barren bit of gravel from one viciously-barbed border fence to the other and entered Tajikistan. The duty officer, a nuggety chap with heavy eyebrows and stubble, welcomed us with a wide grin. He beckoned us to a small concrete hut where we showed him the message from Phil Goff translated into Russian. He signed the record book, stamped our passports, and 15 minutes later we returned across the same bit of dirt to Uzbekistan.

A group of young men in fatigues was now in charge and we pleaded again to bypass a visa stamp. One short fellow with a swarthy, deeply-seamed face left the group and marched over to us, exaggerating his stride to emphasise his importance. He grinned, revealing a gold front tooth, and shook my hand formally. 'Stamp is problem for you,' he said. 'No stamp is even bigger problem for me.' So we lost our visa, but it was a good-natured encounter and ended with everybody smiling broadly, shaking hands and slapping each other on the back. It meant that we wouldn't be able to go to Afghanistan from here as planned. We'd just have to work it in some other time.

On the return journey to Tashkent we stopped to photograph a group of children who had waved vigorously at us from the edge of a cotton field. Uzbekistan is the world's largest producer of cotton, and at harvest time it is customary for children to go to the fields after school to pick cotton. When we asked them what their dream was they chorused, 'We want to go to America.'

57  Kyrgyzstan

Next morning Tashkent' s angular contours were softened by a thick coating of snow. It was still falling heavily as we made our way to the airport to fly to Bishkek in the north of Kyrgyzstan. The flight was an hour late leaving and while were waiting to board the Tupolev (an antediluvian Series 154) we met Patrick Ludgate, a short neat American with remarkably shiny shoes who had an air of influence about him. He was a natural resources consultant – a wanted man in the Stans, which have all been environmentally ravaged.

The flight lasted an hour and it seemed that we were descending for a very long time without any sign of an airport. 'There's no ground,' I said to James, looking out anxiously into grey nothingness. The next second, boof, we landed. The pilot emerged from his cockpit and gave us all a relaxed wave as if to say, 'No problem.'

'These things were flying before I was born,' Patrick assured us. 'They're bulletproof and as safe as houses.'

I hailed a taxi and negotiated a price. At the front door of the hotel the driver demanded twice the agreed rate, which resulted in our having a blazing, nose-to-nose, finger-jabbing row. He backed down and accepted the original fee. With a degree of satisfaction I recounted the story to the receptionist. She smiled indulgently. 'Actually, the real price is half that,' she said, and giggled at the look on my face.

We shuffled to our room to prepare for the next day, feeling dismal; but in the hotel's casino that night we were immensely cheered, not by our winnings, but by the staff who plied us with drinks and gathered around, applauding our every move. We

Kazakhstan Cemetery on the road
from Bishkek to Almaty.

were the only guests in the place. The staff numbered around 20.

As dawn was breaking I peered out the hotel window and my spirits soared. Another coating of snow had dusted the trees overnight and the sky had lost its foreboding leaden look. The town of Bishkek spreads out among spacious parks and attractive buildings. The best-looking building in town was the Russian Orthodox church with ornate white walls and bright blue spires.

Because we could not now go to Afghanistan we decided we had time to drive to Almaty, Kazakhstan, instead of flying. First stop, however, was in downtown Bishkek to pick up our tickets from the Uzbekistan Airways office for the Almaty to Istanbul flight next day. This turned out to be a bizarre experience.

James was met at the door by two flustered-looking women and then the demure, pale-faced Russian at the front desk greeted him apologetically. 'I am very sorry, Mr Irving, but I do not have your tickets. We've had a fire and the computers are down,' she said.

'I'm sorry,' said James. 'When did that happen?'

'Er, now,' she said pointing to a small side room where a

fellow was maniacally discharging a fire extinguisher towards the flames that were licking at his computer.

Our tickets were written out by hand.

58 Kazakhstan

A taxi took us to the border of Kazakhstan about 40 minutes from the city centre where we had to get out and walk. Once we had crossed the border, we jumped aboard a large red bus which was to take us along the old Silk Road, across the steppes of Central Asia to Almaty five hours away. But after one look at the jam of passengers in their creaky leather coats and fur hats, squeezed into narrow seats and juggling with bulging bags of thermos flasks and food parcels, we decided to continue in the taxi.

The land we moved through was flat and featureless except for clumps of bare poplar trees, poor concrete houses and the occasional cemetery. The few battered cars that shared the road had cracked or shattered windscreens. Foraging in the snow were herds of thick-coated cows, small brown horses, donkeys and long-haired goats. Under the Soviets, parts of the Kazakhstan were used for testing nuclear weapons and exiling ethnic minorities. The environment is, by all accounts, exceedingly degraded by toxic chemicals. Where we were it didn't look too bad.

Every 30 kilometres or so was a checkpoint. Constabulary dressed in army gear that looked like left-overs from World War II would cross-examine our driver – obviously about us, as they kept nodding in our direction. Then invariably they would glance at us, grin (often displaying one or two gold-filled teeth), hold out their hands and wheedle:

'Baksheesh, baksheesh.'

'*Bishkek*?' we'd say, playing dumb. '*Nyet Russki*.' Eventually they'd leave, empty-handed. It was easier getting money from the locals.

We pulled into Almaty in the pollution-hazed light of late afternoon and saw to the south of the city the looming shapes of the dramatic Zailiysa Alatau Mountains. They would have formed a spectacular backdrop to the city if we could have seen them without the fog.

Almaty is often described as the Paris of Central Asia. From what we saw it did not live up to that reputation. Nothing on our circuitous route to the hotel (the driver didn't know where he was going) looked anything like the Champs-Élysées. The avenues were long and straight and the architecture, once again, blandly Russian. The city had recently become cosmopolitan with shops, restaurants, casinos and bars catering for foreign traders and financiers who had come here to snatch a slice of the country's mineral pie.

I'd had no idea what to expect of the Stans. These former republics of the USSR are very isolated but, since independence in 1991, have prospered to some extent. Kazakhstan is better-off because it has oil, but there is also ample evidence of hardship.

Kyrgyzstan has nothing to offer except water, and after independence it tried to charge for the water in the rivers that flowed on into Uzbekistan. The Uzbekistanis refused to pay and so Kyrgyzstan stopped importing coal to generate its electricity and built hydro power plants instead. This has left Uzbekistan high and, quite literally, dry.

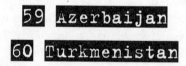

The next morning as we were boarding our flight to Baku, the capital of Azerbaijan, we met Mathew Towse, a lanky, rumpled-looking Southlander who was the area manager for Volvo Trucks and one of five New Zealanders living in Almaty. The flight took us over the desolate moonscape of the Kara Kum Desert of Turkmenistan, which we would cross again later that day when we took a night flight to Ashkabad.

From the air Baku looked as if it was losing its battle with the surrounding desert. Sandy tentacles crept in past patches of vegetation and scattered oil rigs to infiltrate the outskirts of the city. The centuries-old central city, a maze of narrow alleys, domes, arches, palaces, mosques and public buildings in mosaic and ancient stonework, spreads around a natural harbour on the Caspian Sea.

Turkmenistan was another nation for which we had been unable to arrange visas. To get around this we would take a flight leaving Baku at around 10 p.m., fly to Ashkabad, wait for the turnaround and arrive back in Baku at about 2 a.m. Crazy? Of course.

We were flying on Lufthansa. We had to talk hard to convince the ground staff to take us to a place for which we had no visa when we had no luggage and were going to return on the same flight half an hour after we'd landed. It must have looked pretty suspicious, but after we had turned somersaults explaining the reason, we were granted boarding passes. It was a huge relief. On board, the attendants and other passengers were fascinated by our journey and posed for photographs, signed the record book, asked a lot of questions and took photographs of us. And so we had an entertaining time aloft and, when we cheerily waved goodbye to passengers and crew as we left the craft, we felt like departing royalty.

Our arrival had been radioed ahead. When we disembarked the ground crew also welcomed us with high excitement, handshakes, back-slapping, more photographs and our return boarding passes. Then we were handed over to an armed soldier who escorted us military-style to the huge, vacant, very dim transit hall to wait out the hour at the lounge bar. On the wall was an imposing photograph of President Saparmurad Niyazov with a lit cigarette in his hand. He is said to have ordered modernisation of the central city of Ashkabad with new buildings, mosques and boulevards – a move which is seen as a self-aggrandising extravagance that has done little to improve the man in the street's prosperity.

We thought the number of passengers on the flight to Ashkabad was low, but on the return flight in the dead of night there were only about 20 of us. Everyone looked as dazed as we felt. There is something deeply eccentric about flying from Ashkabad to Baku in the middle of the night.

Back in Baku, after a few hours' sleep in a hotel room, we sauntered down Ziverbey Akhmedbeyov Street and Neftchilar Avenue. It was Azerbaijan's Independence Day holiday, and along the waterfront it seemed that every one of the city's 2.5 million residents had decided to promenade beside the sea. Young girls were chaperoned by their mothers, and young men in black suits hung about in groups looking at the young girls.

We pushed our way into an outdoor caravanserai and sat in the cool air overlooking the waterfront. We ordered beer, although lemon tea seemed to be more the national drink, and ate chicken in pita bread. The meal cost us something like $NZ6. Everything here was very reasonably priced, which made it one of the few places in the world where New Zealanders didn't have to shudder at the exchange rate.

But not everybody led the good life in Baku. I brought out a wad of money to count out the bill and was immediately approached by a toothless crone dressed in a headscarf and voluminous skirts. I had money in my hand and it seemed churlish not to give her some. There was an immediate response from the waiter who rushed over and berated the old woman in a tirade which almost certainly meant 'Get lost'. She stood her ground and hurled abuse back at him. We left them to their disagreement.

We really liked what we saw of Baku. It is the port of an oil-rich country, modern and liberal in attitude. Its wide tree-lined boulevards reminded me of a Paris whose buildings hadn't been maintained for the last 80 years. It used to be an important stopover on the Silk Road and is famous for its magnificent carpets and its sturgeon caviare from the Caspian Sea.

Everywhere we went the Azerbaijanis made us feel welcome, and if we asked directions they would personally escort us to wherever we wanted to go. At the local barber's we had not only very classy haircuts and blow-dries but also a relaxing head and shoulder massage, and a whiff of snuff to liven us up thrown in for the price of only a few dollars.

We'd planned to go from Baku to Georgia, Armenia and Iran, but in the morning were told by a local travel agent that visas were now essential to enter Georgia. It was a Friday and a public holiday so we couldn't get visas until Monday, three days later. We headed for Austria instead.

At check-in, the desk clerk looked at me coyly and said, 'The lady down there has sympathy for you.'

There were two ground staff standing further down the counter, one quite pretty, the other an older, tougher-looking woman with two front teeth missing. I questioned the clerk again.

'She desires you.'

'Which one?'

'The old one.'

Just my luck. I walked over to my admirer and put my arm around her. James took a photograph, and everybody laughed.

'You have uplifted our morning,' said the clerk.

77 UNITED KINGDOM

78 NETHERLANDS

75 GERMANY

76 BELGIUM

74 LUXEMBOURG

72 LIECHTENSTEIN

61 AUSTRIA

71 FRANCE

73 SWITZERLAND

70 MONACO

69 San Marino

68 VATICAN CITY

62 BULGARIA

81 PORTUGAL

79 ANDORRA

80 SPAIN

67 ITALY

63 MALTA

64 TUNISIA

66 ALGERIA

65 LIBYA

118

CHAPTER TEN

Europe and North Africa

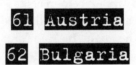

We flew through Istanbul to Vienna, where we'd intended to stay the night. But because we hadn't been able to get to Georgia we were ahead of schedule and decided to visit Sofia in Bulgaria and return to Vienna in time to catch a southward flight to Tunis the next day.

It was afternoon when we arrived in Sofia and we strolled through the city which, although a bit rough around the edges, had retained some of the magnificent historical buildings alongside new retail stores. The fashionable Vitosha Boulevard led to Bulgaria Square, where we sat at an outdoor café in the heavy sulphurous air, ordered a beer and watched the Bulgarians go by.

Bulgaria's transition to democracy has caused high unemployment and high inflation. The country is now plodding towards a better future but the people have had a tough time and it showed in their faces – in the coarse, careworn features of the men and the weary women.

We had dinner in a mehana – a traditional taverna-style restaurant – where we were guided to a cubicle in a dim basement furnished with plain wooden tables. We ate meatballs and chilli penne pasta, with beer and wine. The bill was $NZ18. Inflation has been so rampant here that everything is ridiculously cheap for foreigners.

We left Sofia at dawn, heading back to Vienna in time to catch a flight to Malta.

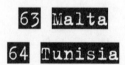

63 Malta
64 Tunisia

Flying south into an oyster-coloured sky we had clear views of the Italian coastline, Sicily and the Mediterranean. We'd intended to stay the night in Malta but when the captain announced that he was flying on to Tunis we decided to continue with him. So when we landed at Valletta we disembarked, passed through immigration, raced to the Air Malta ticketing counter, bought our onward tickets and raced back to the plane waving new boarding passes.

It was late at night in Tunis. The shaggy silhouettes of palm trees contrasted with the smooth brightness of whitewashed buildings, and satellite dishes crowned the roofs of the many high-rise apartments.

At the Hilton Hotel we were assured that we had rooms with premium views. I pulled back the curtains with a flourish next morning to the stunning vista of the yard behind the kitchen strewn with rubbish.

It was 21 October when we made our attempt to get into Libya without visas. James went to Tunis airport mid-morning to try to get us onto a there-and-back flight. He came back several hours later elated.

He had first talked to the station manager and shown him the logbook with the message from Phil Goff written in Arabic. 'It eees possible,' said the manager, who then led him to another official who puffed out his cheeks and made several phone calls. As James waited, a pretty secretary in a short blue skirt eyed him flirtatiously (he thought) as she puffed on a cigarette. The second official got off the phone. 'Is okay,' he said.

That is how we got to the Socialist People's Libyan Arab Jamahiriya – it wasn't much of a visit, but at least we made it.

65 Libya

In the airport at Tripoli we were escorted by the station manager to a less austere than imagined arrivals lounge which was empty of people. A few small glass cabinets displayed some duty-free goods. No alcohol, of course. Libya is 98 percent Arab and Muslim. We had two hours to wait before the plane left again.

It was hard to convince ourselves as we sat listening to the music from *Chariots of Fire* coming through the sound system that we were really in Libya. The men who strolled past us wore western-style dress or khaki uniforms. Most women wore headscarves and only a handful were in full burkha. Libya under Gaddafi has had a policy of liberalisation and although the country has had some bad press in the West, we understood that Tripoli was an urbane city and the people were remarkably hospitable. The airport police, and there were plenty of them, were unarmed.

An immigration officer called Nasser asked us what we were doing. He showed great interest in the record book, signed it for us and posed for photos. 'I am really sorry that you could not get a visa to see more of our country,' he said. 'It is possible, but you have to go through an approved travel company specialising in Libyan travel.' We'd spent five months talking to embassies trying in vain to get information. If we'd known how to get a visa, our experience of Libya could have been a lot more interesting than drumming our heels at the airport.

Back in Tunis, we looked up Rashed Trineche, founder and president of Club International des Grands Voyages (CIGV). This body has an exclusive worldwide membership of people who have travelled to 50 countries or more so that they can exchange contacts and advice: our joining up catapulted the New Zealand membership to two. We arranged to meet Rashed at his *pharmecie* (he was also a chemist), a small understocked shop with three glass cabinets for medicines and potions. On the wall was a large poster of groups of bare-breasted, scantily-clad girls who looked as though they might have come straight from the Moulin Rouge.

Rashed pointed to them. 'Bravo! They are New Zealanders,' he laughed. 'They came here with a show several years ago. Caramba! Very fulsome,' he said, brandishing his hands to make suggestive curves.

His office, just around the corner, was even smaller than the pharmacy and crammed with memorabilia from his travels, the walls adorned with yellowing newspaper clippings and photographs from around the world. 'Caramba!' he boomed. 'I've been to 110 countries, including New Zealand!'

While we signed the papers, Rashed held animated conversations on the phone, guffawing, gesticulating, running his fingers through his tousled grey hair and bellowing 'Caramba' or 'Bravo' after every statement. He was short, but huge on energy and enthusiasm. The more that was going on around him the happier he seemed to be.

Tunis, now home to a French/Arab culture, has been occupied

over the last 3000 years by Phoenicians, Romans, Byzantines, Arabs and Ottomans. It's a fascinating city. We tried to get into Medina, the city's cultural heart, but late in the afternoon the traffic was so congested that we'd have missed our flight to Algiers. Instead we drove to the ruins of Carthage, which was sacked by the Romans about 100 BC. There is little of beauty left. We walked around the once-grand amphitheatre and the ruins of the residential area and public baths. Most interesting in a grisly way was the Sanctuary of Tophet, which was only excavated in 1921. Pits, overgrown with grass, indicated the places where Carthaginian nobles had killed and roasted their children to appease the deities.

 66 Algeria

It was a brief flight from Tunis to Algiers on Algeria's Mediterranean coast. On the ground we were met by Krino Bouhacira, an Algerian who looked like a swarthy Humphrey Bogart. He signed the record book and issued us with new boarding passes.

The security at Algiers airport was detailed. Everyone's bags were checked by hand as well as by screening, and we wouldn't have wanted to mess with the heavily-armed guards who were positioned around the plane while it was on the tarmac.

We asked Krino if there had been a lot of trouble or if they were expecting it. 'No. No trouble when you have security like this,' he said, broadening his grin to display a row of large tobacco-stained teeth.

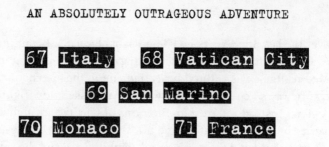

Our quick dip into northern Africa was over. We flew on to Rome and took a train and then a taxi to Vatican City, at 44 hectares the smallest nation in the world. Rome was as chaotic and stimulating as ever. At Vatican City we joined a queue which was 10 wide and seemingly a kilometre long, which put us off having the book signed by a Swiss Guard. We took photographs and approached an American couple to ask them to sign the book to prove that we'd been there. The wife, a haughty woman whose hair stood up stiffly in a chemical-forced bouffant, wouldn't have a bar of us, even when we explained that we weren't trying to sell her anything. Her husband Todd, a pleasant little man with thick-rimmed glasses, was more accommodating. We convinced him we were, at worst, Kiwis on a bit of a lark. He still looked dubious but signed the book.

From Rome there began a stamp-collecting, whistle-stop race through several European countries, dashing from train to taxi to plane with hardly time to sleep or eat or ruminate on where we actually were. No wonder Todd thought we were odd.

First we travelled by train to Rimini so that we could get to San Marino, then a madcap stop at Monte Carlo in Monaco which, if we'd blinked, we would have missed. Luckily James was alert enough to drag us out of the train and onto the station platform where Giordan, the station manager, just had time to sign the book. Then he blew his whistle, we jumped back on the train and we were off to Nice. A blurry shot of signage on the Monte Carlo station also proved we had been there.

Nice was well into its off season. It looked empty and rather

James, St Peter's Square, Vatican City.

seedy. But that unkind assessment could have been due to our exhaustion from the speed of our travels. James reckoned I was grumpy. I reckoned *he* was grumpy. The peevish, sour-faced little man in command at the hotel did nothing to help. The room was the size of a pantry, we'd been given a double bed when we had booked a twin, the restaurant was closed, the club sandwich from room service was disgusting and the prices were exorbitant. I looked at James who was stoically eating his sandwich and decided I did not want to spend that night anywhere near him. I ordered another room. James thought I was being overly reactive . . . and so it went on.

After seven hours' sleep well away from each other's breathing we felt better, although the atmosphere between us was still tense. We had to be up very early again to catch our flight to Zurich, which would connect us to a train that would take us to Chur, near the Swiss mountain village of Flims where our mutual first cousin Stephen Hunter and his partner Therese lived.

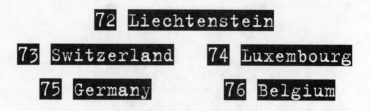

Our plans crashed like a motorway pile-up. We figured that the one airline in the world that you could trust checking your bags in with was Swiss Air. We had distinctly seen our bags come out to the plane on the luggage trolley in Nice, but while we landed safely in Zurich our bags did not. They had stayed on the tarmac in Nice.

We had to hang around for four hours for the next Swiss Air flight from Nice to come in, so we missed our train connection to Chur. In Zurich it was about eight degrees, drizzling and, as far as I was concerned, bloody miserable.

Bags retrieved, I phoned Stephen and rearranged our rendezvous. We travelled by train from Zurich to Sargans. Then we jumped onto a bus and journeyed to the tiny nation of Liechtenstein high in the Alps, east of the Rhine River, where we spent 20 minutes in the tourist office and despite our protests that related to only having small bags we came out laden with information.

Stephen plucked us off the bus and whizzed us through Chur to his mountain village of Flims, at the base of a skifield. It was a great relief to spend a night in their chalet. We sat looking out the windows at the lofty snow-capped mountain and ate home-cooked pork.

Early next morning we were off to Chur station waving our Eurail passes for a seven-day charge through Europe, blinking occasionally to prove we were still alert. First to Luxembourg, via France through dense sheets of rain, where we tried to organise our onward journey through Germany and Belgium to the

Netherlands. It was cold, and the overhead heating in the station's ticket office blasting down probably accounted for the clerk's red face, glowing pate and addled brain. He *thought* that a train went to Cologne next day and on to Belgium, and he *thought* it continued onto Amsterdam.

'Hmm,' I said, 'you've *thought* that through well.' He didn't get it.

Thinking, however, had little to do with what actually happened next day. We found that we could go through Trier to Cologne, Bad Aachen, Brussels and onto Amsterdam in one day, and booked the tickets.

After Trier we slid smoothly through the steep vine-lined valley of the Rhine River to Cologne, where we changed trains and had just enough time to grab a curry wurst and catch another train to Bad Aachen. At the station we noticed that a high wind was bending the trees and grabbing viciously at the sides of the station building but we thought little of it. Ten minutes out of the city travelling north, the train suddenly stopped. 'Technical problem,' we were told, and then we heard that a furious storm was battling across Western Europe. It had ripped up a tree out of the ground and thrown it across the railway track in front of the train.

Rumour raged as fast as the storm, which was now a hurricane: fences and foliage were torn to shreds; roofs were disappearing; there were several trees across our track, as well as a tangle of telephone wire.

Half an hour of this and then the train reversed back to Bad Aachen, where a portion of the station's roof had been dislodged and sirens were screeching. We debouched, huddled in the station for about two hours, and then struggled through the teeth of the wind to a chartered bus which took us to Welkenraedt in Belgium, where we caught a train to Brussels.

James and I had booked a hotel in Amsterdam. When we rang to cancel, the receptionist informed us that no trains in the Netherlands were operating and Amsterdam airport was closed.

The scene at Brussel's Gare Midi was chaos. Hundreds of passengers' travel plans were disrupted, and everyone was looking for a bed for the night. We were so tired we were almost out of fight, but summoned enough strength to grab the last spare room at the Ibis Hotel opposite the station.

77 United Kingdom

The next day we travelled by train on the trans-Chunnel Eurostar to London for a desperately-needed four days on familiar ground, visiting friends and resting. Amsterdam would have to come later. Our only pressing task in London was to get those elusive Georgian visas.

We met consul Konstantin Surguladze at the embassy who told us he knew of a Georgian who was cycling to all nations of the world. We had some strong competition.

Two days later we went again to collect the visas and were met by Ambassador Mamatsashvili, who invited us into his office and called for a bottle of Georgian wine. He jovially toasted the Quest, Georgia, New Zealand, good fortune and good health and we clinked our glasses. We liked Ambassador Mamatsashvili immensely. A portly, jovial man with a generous smile, he loved to talk about Georgia, a wonderful country, he said, which grew citrus, tea and plenty of grapes for the wine. By the time the cork popped on the second bottle he was regaling us with Georgian jokes, like this one:

Georgian province declares war on China. When the Chinese hear this, they say, 'Where is this place?' And when they find out that Georgia is a tiny country on the Black Sea they send a delegation of generals to placate the dissidents.

At the conference the Chinese delegates ask, 'How many soldiers do you have in your army?'

The Georgians reply, 'Fifty thousand.'

Consul Konstantin Surguladze (left) and Ambassador
Mamatsashvili (right), at the Georgian embassy.

'Do you realise that in China we have millions?'

'Oh dear,' say the Georgians. 'Where are we going to bury
them all?'

The ambassador doubles over with laughter. We think we are
going to like Georgia.

78 The Netherlands
79 Andorra

Two days later, on a clear autumn day, we left London on KLM
and skimmed over neatly furrowed fields and orderly roads to
land in Amsterdam. After clearing Customs we lay by the fountain at the front of the terminal soaking up the warmth of the
sun. Much warmth was also displayed by a number of couples
around the fountain clinched in passionate embraces. Maybe the
sun does that to people in this part of the world.

On the flight to Toulouse, the captain was a former Ansett
pilot. She invited me to the cockpit for the record book signing

Flight from Amsterdam to Toulouse. Captain Deborah
Lawrie and Co-pilot Melanie de Vries.

and a photograph. We then took a taxi across the city to Central
Station to catch a southbound train for L'Hospitalet near the
border with Andorra and then a bus to the country's main town,
Andorra la Vella.

The dark of night and a heavy fog camouflaged just how
steeply the road carved through the Pyrenees mountains, but
next morning we were treated to a clear bright sunlight illumi-
nating the shoulders of the dramatic swirl of peaks surrounding
the town.

Andorra is a tiny princedom, only about 35 kilometres across,
and what it lacks in size it makes up for in other ways: the best
skifields, the most dramatic mountain scenery in the Pyrenees,
and some of the best shopping in Europe. Electronics, alcohol
and luxury goods are tax-free. In fact, Andorra la Vella is really
one huge bazaar of retail shops stuffed with goods that pander to
the wants of the country's French and Spanish neighbours, who
pour in there to search for good-quality bargains.

The power of a good deal was demonstrated next day at the

start of a four-day public holiday in Spain, when we left in a minibus to drive to Barcelona. The traffic coming into Andorra la Vella was nose-to-tail, creeping along at no more than 10 km/h and stretching back for 150 kilometres. We were thankful to be moving freely on the other side of the road – downhill through the verdant hills all the way to Barcelona.

80 Spain
81 Portugal

In Barcelona we drove straight to the airport through an unromantic industrial area west of the city and flew to Lisbon. There we had an enforced three-day break while we caught up with ourselves. I was way behind with reports, and emails were pouring in. The second record book was being couriered to us from New Zealand but by the Day of the Dead, when Portuguese take a holiday to visit their cemeteries, it had still not arrived. My own cemetery at home had a few issues I needed to deal with, and James was rushing from embassies to airline offices rearranging the schedule in preparation for our launch into Africa and an uncertain future.

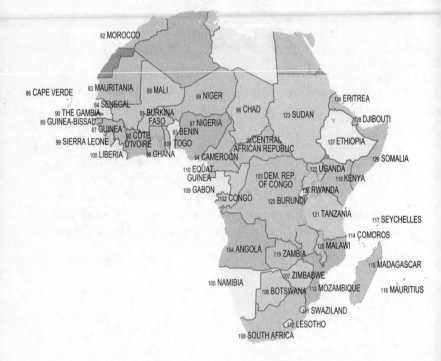

82 MOROCCO

86 CAPE VERDE 83 MAURITANIA 88 MALI 89 NIGER 124 ERITREA

90 THE GAMBIA 84 SENEGAL 91 BURKINA 96 CHAD 123 SUDAN 128 DJIBOUTI
85 GUINEA-BISSAU FASO
87 GUINEA 97 NIGERIA 127 ETHIOPIA
99 SIERRA LEONE 92 CÔTE 93 BENIN
D'IVOIRE 101 TOGO 95 CENTRAL
100 LIBERIA 98 GHANA AFRICAN REPUBLIC 129 SOMALIA
94 CAMEROON
110 EQUAT. 122 UGANDA
GUINEA 103 DEM. REP. 118 KENYA
109 GABON OF CONGO 126 RWANDA
102 CONGO 125 BURUNDI
121 TANZANIA 117 SEYCHELLES
114 COMOROS
104 ANGOLA 120 MALAWI
119 ZAMBIA 115 MADAGASCAR
105 NAMIBIA 107 ZIMBABWE 116 MAURITIUS
106 BOTSWANA 113 MOZAMBIQUE
111 SWAZILAND
112 LESOTHO
108 SOUTH AFRICA

132

Top left Thanks for the cigarette – we'll be going then. Bitola, Macedonia. *Top right* Georgian town towards the Armenian border. Wedding dresses on display no matter what the weather. *Bottom left* Open-air market, downtown Tbilisi, Georgia. When the plucked turkeys are sold, the live ones soon end up in their place. *Bottom right* If there was a broken seat on any plane, John was seated in or near it.

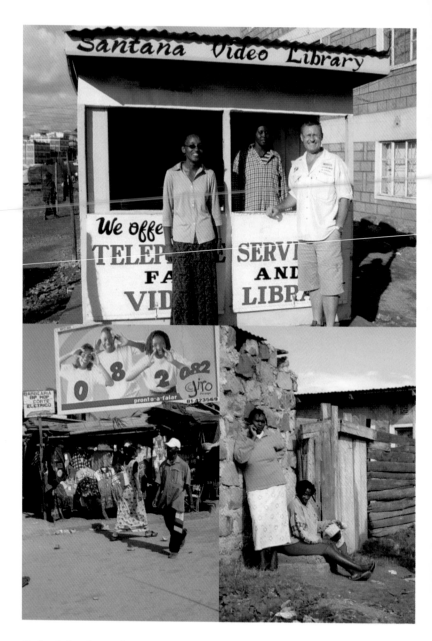

Top Small shop that was big on services. Caroline Kabena, Githurai, on the outskirts of Nairobi, Kenya. *Bottom left* New technology with shops that haven't changed in centuries. Main retail street, Quelimane, Mozambique. *Bottom right* Checking out the photo shoot outside Caroline's home, Githurai, Nairobi, Kenya.

Top Our constant saviour, Phil Goff's letter and its author, pre-departure. *Bottom left* What you can't do is made clear, Palm Beach, Lome, Togo. *Bottom right* Typical beach scene, Conakry, Guinea.

Top The constant necessity of updating the website meant little rest in Fiji. *Bottom* Finalists in the Mr and Miss Competition, Palau.

Top Mohammed at Bahrain International Airport after helping us cross into Saudi Arabia. *Bottom left* Guam Hotel grounds after the December 2002 typhoon. *Bottom right* Captain Jim McIntire (back left), (ISM) Noella Mowerton (middle left), James (front) and crew on Continental flight CS7 Narita to Guam.

Top left Kolkata road scene with the rickshaw doubling as taxi and truck. *Top right* Between-match entertainment at the Pakistani wrestling tournament. The stone weighs 200 kg. *Bottom left* Miss Park with us on the Panmunjom border with North Korea behind. *Bottom right* Choeung EK Genocidal Centre.

Top left Proudly displaying the sponsors' logos beside the Ljubljana River, Ljubljana, Slovenia. *Top right* The Tromostovje (triple bridge) leading to Preseren Square and the Franciscan Church, Ljubljana, Slovenia. *Bottom* John's wife Anna and daughter Nic at Giza, Cairo, amid negotiations for the sale of Anna – it got to 1 million camels.

Top right The only thing working in the Central Square on a Sunday, St Kitts. *Top left* The other side of San Salvador – the downtown shopping centre. *Bottom right* On the road to Maracas Beach, Trinidad. *Bottom left* James' fascination with ferrets (odd hairstyles) demanded that all ferreterias be identified.

CHAPTER ELEVEN

NORTH AND WEST AFRICA

82 Morocco

On the morning of the day we were to leave Lisbon the record book had still not arrived. We cursed TNT and chased around making phone calls and scanning drop-off points. At around 4 p.m. the parcel was found at TNT's head office at Lisbon Airport where it had been held up by Customs. Clutching its contents we flew on to Casablanca, arriving late at night.

When I pulled back the curtains in the morning I was greeted by a breathtaking view over the old city, the adjoining harbour and the enormous domes and towers of Mosque Hassan II, which dominated the coast and cast a protective shadow over the shortbread-coloured cram of flat-roofed buildings. What an introduction to Africa!

Forward bookings for Africa had been impossible because

enquiries went unanswered and airline schedules constantly changed. We were going to have to travel that huge continent on a wing and a prayer. Most of the day in Morocco was spent at a travel agent's making bookings for the West Africa sectors, an exercise which became so complex that we ran late leaving for the airport in time to catch the flight to Mauritania that evening.

It started to get really serious when a squabble broke out between our taxi driver and another. They danced about shouting and brandishing their arms. The minutes slipped by. And then one of them bundled us into a 30-year-old Mercedes which had to be hot-wired five times before the engine kicked into life. With diesel fumes pouring behind us we careered down the road vibrating up to a top speed of 100 km/h.

The flight had closed. We begged the young Moroccan woman at the check-in counter to let us on. I hauled out our wad of tickets pretending that they were for the next 50 sectors and waved it in front of her. 'If we don't get on we'll miss all these flights,' I whined.

Her eyes widened. 'Okay, okay,' she said, and processed our boarding cards.

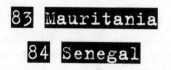

83 Mauritania
84 Senegal

And so to Nouakchott, where we taxied to the Mercure Hotel. 'You're booked for tomorrow,' the receptionist said curtly. 'We're full. Go to the Houda down the road.'

By name it sounded more like a brothel than a hotel, but it turned out to be pleasantly comfortable. Because Mauritania is Muslim and the bar was dry, we opened a bottle of wine we had with us and were offered glasses by the only other person there, a man in a flowing white bou-bou (a long flowing robe that protects the wearer from sand and heat) and carefully wound turban.

Mohammed Amara, a Mauritanian who had been educated in Britain, had just returned from working in Ghana. He told us how after independence from France, Senegal and Mauritania split into two, which left Mauritania without a capital city. 'The president put his finger on the map and announced, "Here will be the nation's capital",' he said. 'It was just a small village of tents then. So no one comes here expecting historical buildings.'

I asked him if I could pay him to show us around next day.

'I will be delighted,' he said. 'But I will not hear of you paying.'

He arrived to collect us next morning as we were having breakfast and looked longingly at our plates of cheese and cold meats. For him it was the first day of Ramadan, when Muslims may not eat or drink between sunrise and sunset.

The buildings he drove us past had all been erected in the last 40 years. Tentacles of sand everywhere indicated how fast the Sahara Desert was encroaching: on the city's outskirts square wooden dwellings not much bigger than car cases were set on the sand. There was not a road, a blade of grass or a single tree in sight.

'Mauritanians were nomads,' said Mohammed, 'but drought has driven them to these slums. Like many West African countries, Mauritania is collapsing because of drought, war and corruption. Thousands of lives are threatened by famine.'

My large breakfast rumbled in my stomach.

'But Americans are here and there's a rumour that oil has been found. If it's true it will change the city forever.'

We drove to the coastal fishing village of Plage des Pecheurs where slim long-boats were returning with large catches of fish and others putting out to sea. They looked far from seaworthy but balanced on the beach they were a picturesque sight. Any pictures I took, however, had to be furtive. The fishermen had a strong aversion to being photographed. Maybe they considered it bad luck – or perhaps it was because I smoked, which was, I later discovered, an irreverent thunderclap during Ramadan.

We drove across the bare sand to look at camels and sheep which had been herded into rough pens ready to be sold for post-sunset feasting. And then, close to a ramshackle group of huts, our taxi became sand-bogged to the axles. It was quickly dug out by a gang of ragged, mid-adolescent boys who just happened to be around. 'They scrape a living waiting for people like us,' said Mohammed.

Back in the city we stopped at Air Senegal's office and told the elderly male receptionist that we needed tickets to Senegal for later that day. 'Oh,' he said, calculating far too quickly, 'economy is full.'

We didn't argue. I bought two business-class tickets, and at the airport an hour later thanked Mohammed profusely before boarding a cramped little Air Senegal Dash 8-300. Economy of course was nearly empty. Lesson learnt!

Dakar was 1874 kilometres to the south. When we landed we unfurled and walked like bent bananas to immigration to present the visas which had taken most of the year 2002 to obtain.

Formerly an urbane French administrative centre, Dakar is surrounded by desert, but the streets lined with trees, pubs and cafés still lend it a certain style. We had decided to make this our base for the next few days, so we overnighted in a middle-range hotel and early in the morning were back at the airport.

Outside the Dakar Airport terminal we were mobbed by insistent, scruffy, barefoot men who brayed that they were magnificent tour guides and could show us anything in Dakar. I shouted, 'Tell us where the Air Senegal offices is.' The clamour died. We shoved through their ranks and quite by chance fell through the door of the Air Senegal office, startling the tall young woman behind the desk.

Yes, she could make our bookings, but no she couldn't issue the tickets – the printer was broken. And unfortunately, no, she couldn't take a credit card because the machine was not working.

Planning to get to Cape Verde had been one of the nightmares of the Quest. In Europe it had looked as if the only option would be to fly there and back again in the dead of night. And then at the last minute we found a new schedule that went from Senegal to Guinea-Bissau and on to Cape Verde.

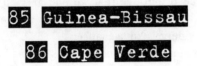

85 Guinea-Bissau
86 Cape Verde

It was a long flight out to the islands. We first looked down on the undeveloped estuaries, islands and mangroves of Guinea-Bissau then landed at its capital, Bissau, which is surrounded by low-lying swamps.

The flight attendant let me disembark to have a cigarette, but the tarmac was a no-smoking zone. I went up to two security guards. 'I really need a smoke,' I mimed. They beckoned me to follow them to their hut at the edge of the tarmac and we all lit up amid much miming, grinning and handshaking. We could have been behind the bike sheds at school.

Cape Verde, an isolated and fragmented archipelago 560 kilometres off the coast of West Africa, is popular with European package holidaymakers because fine weather is almost guaranteed. The islands suffer from chronic lack of water and sometimes famine: the last time there had been a drop of rain was four years before we arrived.

The international airport is on the flat island of Sal. Most other islands are hilly but their landscapes, from aloft, were devoid of foliage and as barren as the moon. A cabby who spoke Crioulo (a mix of Portuguese and Creole) and excellent English delivered us to the Oasis Bellorizonte Hotel, which was a series of cabins and run like a Butlins holiday camp. All the in-house rules and timetables made our overnight stay rather tense; and when we were woken at the ungodly hour of 3 a.m. to catch a 5 a.m. flight back to Dakar, we were not in a holiday mood.

87 Guinea

On 7 November we flew southeast to Conakry. The immigration officer refused to believe that we had arrived as tourists — terrorists, more likely. He also thought we were asking for permanent residency. Not a chance.

I explained our mission again and he flashed his teeth at me, planted a stamp in our passports and handed them back with a wink and a nod, as if to say, 'I know what you are really up to'.

Within three seconds of meeting us, our taxi driver wanted to know how we could help him get out of Guinea. He gave us what he called a 'highlights' tour of the city — except there were none.

From the air, Conakry, which spread-eagles over a peninsula, had looked tidy enough, but on the ground it looked sad and accidental. The jungle was reclaiming anything that stood unattended, and the few buildings which couldn't be described as lean-to or shack were in a terrible state of disrepair. This was a city on its knees — a place of degrading poverty and lost hope.

I was horrified by the numb misery and deprivation, the lack of the basics of life which we saw on the side of the choked road that led to the port and downtown, particularly the round-eyed children who squatted in the roadside dust within inches of passing vehicles.

Some industry was evidenced by its appalling effect on the environment. Stacks belched black smoke of such evil composition that it made our eyes water and breathing difficult. Guinea exports a large percentage of the world's high-grade bauxite. Obviously most people never get to see any profit.

The beaches lining the isthmus were covered in festering rubbish. A few rotten-looking boats were pulled up where people still bathed in the fetid water and, worse still, fished. Anyone who just complains about his or her lot should be sent

Conakry, Guinea.

to Conakry for just an hour. They would never complain again.

Our last view of it was from the safety of our plane. As we taxied down the runway, out of the port window we saw a group of men washing themselves in a filthy ditch and staring up at us without expression. They were stark naked.

88 Mali
89 Niger

We overnighted in Dakar again and next day took off to land at Bamako, Mali's capital, where other than descending the stairs to touch the tarmac we stayed on the plane. Mali is land-locked and one of the five poorest nations in the world. From the air it looked like a vast sandpit, with huts occasionally scattered around like hunched beetles.

Niger doesn't look much better from the air. In the fading light we could just make out the darkening desert pitted with wide stony basins. At Niamey Airport we needed boarding passes for a return flight to Bamako and Dakar. A woman took us to a type of cowshed and introduced us to the station manager, also her husband, who issued our boarding passes. Our exit back to the plane was blocked by Sergeant-Major Maman Moussa Kane Dit Teacher. He looked frighteningly surly and jabbered in French to the effect that we shouldn't be in the country because we didn't have visas. I showed him the French translation of Phil Goff's message. He followed every line with his finger, muttering, 'Oui, oui, oui,' and then looked up, beamed his approval and escorted us to the plane. We flew back to Dakar.

90 The Gambia

Banjul was only a two-hour flight away, and looking down we could see the thin slivers of land on each side of the Gambia River, which is all there is of this former British colony.

Banjul, the capital, is at the river's mouth on the Atlantic, and that's where we landed, walked into the arrivals hall, gulped down a beer, and departed. I thought of the early missionaries who, charged with saving the ungodly, were dropped off at miserably deprived and remote spots along the Gambia River and, more often than not, were never seen again. Though far from converted, I did offer up a grateful utterance for the blessings of modern machinery as we slid into the sky towards our last night in Dakar.

91 Burkina Faso

On 13 November we left Senegal and flew east to Ouagadougou where Andy Cole, a New Zealander whom we'd met on the Internet, was waiting for us at the airport. He lived there with his Welsh wife Lara, who worked for the UN World Food Programme. The Coles' neighbours, missionaries Tina and Dave, were also New Zealanders and joined us for drinks on the patio, which was impenetrably swathed in mosquito netting.

We learned something of the ways of Africa and life in Burkina Faso that night: the country had in the past endured many coups and random executions and yet the people, half of them Roman Catholic and half Muslim, have retained a remarkably happy attitude. Being good Kiwis we also lamented at length the All Blacks' loss to England the previous day.

Andy returned us to the airport at 6.30 the next morning after a brief tour around Ouagadougou, which is pretty much bang in the middle of the country. It has few epic monuments or buildings but the streets are wide and shady and, despite the country's poverty, the town is known for its film and art festivals, lively nightclubs, cafés and startling number of bicycles. Some years before, then-Chairman Sankhara had gone to China. On his return, he decreed that the bicycle was to be the transport system of Ouagadougou, and whirling wheels still clogged the flat straight roads of the city.

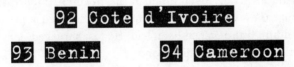

92 Cote d'Ivoire
93 Benin   94 Cameroon

In an Air Burkina Fokker 28-100, we rose above Ouagadougou and turned south towards Abidjan and the turmoil of civil war in the Ivory Coast. Whatever we might have seen of the city below us remained a mystery because the plane's windows had evidently been scrubbed at some time with a wire brush. The only glimpse of it was through a few square centimetres of unmarked glass at the base of an already low-slung window. The cabin crew probably thought we were vomiting as we bent down to peer through the pin-hole of clear glass.

The equally little we spied of Abidjan as we came into land looked like the pilot's shoulder lapels, worn and a little frayed around the edges. We had been fretting about going to Cote d'Ivoire for weeks, anxiously listening to reports from CNN that told us that foreigners had been ordered to leave and that two days prior, there had been heavy gunfire in the streets of Abidjan.

I said to James, 'Let's not get fancy about this. If things look dodgy we should just stay at the airport and keep our heads down.'

The first person we saw after immigration was a sharp-looking African in a smart grey suit who beamed a welcome. 'Tell me truthfully,' I said. 'Is it okay to go into the city?'

'Of course,' he said, looking a bit taken aback.

I tried again. 'With all the mayhem here, you still say it's really quite safe?'

'Of course,' he said, more emphatically. 'There has been no trouble.'

It was rather like driving into a small well-ordered French provincial town. The streets were about as calm and orderly as the suburbs on a Saturday afternoon. I was almost disappointed.

After a very civilised lunch at the Novotel Hotel, I walked through the streets to find a barber. As he snipped at my locks I asked him if things had been bad. He just shrugged. Maybe he didn't understand the question.

After eight hours we went back to the airport to fly to Accra in Ghana. Or so we thought. There was no sign on the monitor of the Air Ivoire's scheduled departure at 5 p.m. We hastened to the ticketing counter which was manned by a fat, middle-aged woman. 'Your flight has departed,' she said in a chastising tone, sucking in her rubbery lips in disapproval. 'It left late at 1500 hours.'

'What?' squeaked James, incredulous. 'Look!' he said jabbing at his ticket. 'It's due to go at 17.10. It's left early!'

She leaned her fat arms on the counter, looked balefully at us with piercing black eyes and yelled: 'It was *late*. It was meant to go at 12.30, so it was *late*.' She spun around, turning her back to us.

YAK-40, waiting for the mother of the wife of
President, Douala.

We were stunned. I hammered on the glass partition. *'C'est impossible!'* I shouted, feeling ridiculous.

Fearing the worst, the woman called the station manager. 'The plane has gone,' he said slowly as if he thought we were slightly retarded.

'The next flight to Accra,' added Madame Podge, 'will not be for another three days.' A sardonic grin flashed across her face.

Baring my teeth in what I hoped looked like a smile, I asked if we could possibly use our existing full-fare ticket as part-payment for another flight.

'No.'

'Then do you accept credit cards for payment?'

'No.'

'Are there any seats on Air Ivoire to anywhere today?'

'Douala only,' she said.

Happily we could use our Visa cards to extract money from the airport's bank and, with a barrowload of local currency, we returned to Madame Podge and booked for Douala. Her efficiency matched her mood. Our names were wrong, the flight details were wrong, the time of departure was wrong. If she had anything to do with it, no wonder the first flight had left *early*.

AN ABSOLUTELY OUTRAGEOUS ADVENTURE

Delivered to the tarmac next to the Fokker 23-4000 bound for Douala, we hung back to enjoy for a moment a cooling breeze. The sky was thunderous: great black clouds had gathered for a monsoonal downpour. Passengers were allowed onto the plane in groups of threes, so that their mountainous piles of cabin baggage could be stowed in an orderly fashion. This entailed shoving and poking at voluminous bags which were obviously not going to fit in the overhead locker, and then trying the locker next door which was, of course, exactly the same size.

When the luggage had been squeezed into every nook and cranny we sat waiting for an hour in the atmosphere of a sauna. The heat was incredible. The lone steward tried to placate the restless, sweating passengers, racing up and down the aisle looking as if he was melting while he handed out tissues and water. His sterling efforts couldn't stop us voting Air Ivoire the worst airline in the world.

Our only stop on the way was at Cotonou in Benin, a small country on the Gulf of Guinea where voodooism is still widely practised and from where around 10,000 slaves were shipped to Haiti in the 18th century. There have been more coups here than in any other country on the continent, but tourists still come from Europe to swan around the golden beaches of its Atlantic coastline.

The only place we swanned around was in the Fokker while we waited once again in a sauna for our flight to continue. When we finally looked down on Douala in Cameroon our greatest relief was that it marked the end of our relationship with Air Ivoire.

Douala was the hub from which, over the next few days, we would make our sorties into the dodgy countries of Central Africa. Our initial impressions of the city were mixed. The weather was still insufferably hot, the airport was grimy and our taxi driver drove like a maniac. But it looked in reasonable shape until we turned off the main road and large potholes started appearing, some as wide as a car and filled with water.

Because of Air Ivoire's mixed-up schedule we had a multi-entry visa but it was not valid for another six days. We were making five entrances and exits from Douala, and without a current visa we had to do a lot of fast-talking each time, including 'accidentally' banging my head on one of the steel bars of a booth and dropping to the floor 'Hollywood' style. Fearing the worst the officer quickly stamped our passports.

We'd booked into Le Meridien Hotel in town where the friendliest faces were those of the hookers lingering around the entrance. One mountainous black woman in a red dress, with thick red lips to match, tottered out from the group extending her arms towards me. 'C'mon dooorling,' she said. I fled to the safety of the hotel's security guard, who demanded money. I fled again.

But it was the surly attitude of the staff and the grubby under-serviced rooms that made the place undesirable. We determined to move out next day. Douala was another unattractive, run-down former French colonial town. In the torpor of the hot sticky climate, goods were slowly moved about, balanced on heads, bicycles or in battered utes. Muggings and banditry we were told made it unwise to go out at night.

95 Central African Republic
96 Chad

We escaped from Le Meridien next morning to fly to the Central African Republic and back, stopping off in Chad. At the Cameroon Airlines check-in the desk clerk, a doe-eyed young woman, stared at my ticket with an anxious frown. We needed three different boarding passes to make the round trip. 'Why do you go there like this?' she asked. 'Where is your luggage?' She went away to consult.

We became anxious that they would not take us at all, so we

Central African
Republic –
immigration
officials.

changed our story. 'We are just going to Bangui and we travel light,' I said. Still looking suspicious, she gave us a hand-written boarding pass.

We had a visa for the Central African Republic but decided not to overnight there as there seemed very little to tempt us, so we just touched down in Bangui, the capital, and took a photograph to prove it.

Those three flights were the most pointless we made on the Quest. In the space of six hours, after a delayed departure from Douala, we had ticked off two more nations – Central African Republic and Chad – and could report almost nothing about them. At both airports we merely touched the tarmac, took photographs and found witnesses to sign the record book. Looking down on Chad we saw yet another huge expanse of sand.

97 Nigeria

98 Ghana

Cameroon Airlines departed from Douala the next morning, hours late again. And when we were 20,000 feet in the air the captain announced that this direct flight to Lagos in Nigeria was now going to Abidjan first.

Delays and changed schedules are integral to getting around African-style. In Cameroon, air travel and all forms of transport are frequently disrupted, particularly at that time of the year when the harmattan winds blow sand from the Sahara, blasting everything in their path and turning the air grey with gritty dust.

So it wasn't all that surprising that what had started out as a one-hour flight took eight. Or that when we arrived in Lagos the flight we'd booked to take us on to Accra had not yet left the place it was coming from. Far from missing it, we had an hour to relax in the departure hall.

Around thirty percent of the population of Africa lives in Nigeria, and it seemed as if they were all at Lagos airport. We ventured outside the terminal and were surrounded by a throng of well-wishers who had only two things on their minds: could we get them out of Nigeria, and please tell the world that everything in Nigeria is 'just fine'.

Back in the queue to board the plane we met Herb Giebel, an American doctor and missionary who had suffered the long flight to Lagos with us. He ran the Seventh-Day Adventist Hospital in Ile-Ife, a town north of Lagos. The 146-bed hospital caters to the locals as best it can, though it is apparently not much more than a corrugated lean-to. The majority of his patients have Aids, Aids-related health problems, or are the survivors of car accidents.

Finally, on the third attempt, we arrived late at night in Ghana's very civilised capital Accra and in a state of advanced exhaustion drove straight to the hotel. In the van with us was a well-dressed, handsome Liberian woman who was returning to Ghana from Minneapolis to uplift her three children. During the civil war in Liberia, the family had fled to Ghana as refugees. After three years she had been given an entry visa to the United States where she battled to get residency permits for the rest of her family. She did not know what had happened to her husband. 'The permits took five years,' she told us without a hint of bitterness.

The next day was our first day off in weeks and gave us a chance to catch up with chores, get tickets organised and enjoy the facilities of the recently refurbished Novotel. Accra was the best African city we'd been in so far, a clean, English-speaking, former British colony. We saw new cars, not one of which had a broken windscreen; the Internet came to life the minute I hit the key; road rules and traffic lights were observed; the buildings were maintained; and the police did not appear to be on the take.

99 Sierra Leone
100 Liberia

While I battled with the website diary updates, James went early to the airport to arrange bookings for a flight west to Sierra Leone for later that day. It was fearsomely hot. I arrived to find him looking as if he'd been dipped in a river and put through a combine harvester, but he was clutching two Ghana Airways tickets.

We took the bus to the plane, boarded, found our seats, stowed our luggage, sat down and then were told to disembark. Our DC9 had been filled with the wrong fuel and we would have to wait until its tanks were drained and filled again. That took longer than the actual flight.

The eventual descent into Freetown revealed the extent of the UN peacekeeping presence in Sierra Leone. Even though the 10-year civil war had ended in an exhausted mutual capitulation in January 2002, a 17,000-strong force remained and their armoury — the white-painted tanks, tents, helicopters, Lear jets and old Russian transport planes — was impressive. Ours was the only non-white and non-UN plane on the tarmac. We were not sure if this brought us comfort or concern.

We'd thought at one stage we might get to Sierra Leone by hiring a car in Conakry in Guinea and driving south to the border. That plan had been extremely naïve. As we flew in we saw that the roads had been broken up by huge holes with tyre tracks around them. But Freetown itself, built on the hills leading up from an enclosed harbour, looked delightful, and it was only timing that prevented us from overnighting there.

We flew southeast to Monrovia in Liberia, our 100th nation. It was dusk as we descended, which to some extent softened the worst features of the run-down building that served as the terminal. Frankly, I've seen better shearing sheds.

We'd had our passports stamped in Freetown even though we didn't leave the airport and I decided to do the same here. I left the plane and presented my passport to an official dressed in a torn and frayed T-shirt at one of the grimy counters in the terminal.

'I would like a stamp,' I said, 'but I will not be entering the country.'

He was a tall man with a few black wisps of beard and bad breath. His ebony skin dripped beads of perspiration. He took the passport and slowly, page by page, investigated its contents. 'It is illegal,' he said in halting English, 'but possible.' He looked at me meaningfully. In other words and after a hastened negotiation, $US15. I got my stamp and turned to race back to the plane. The exit door was closed and the way barred by the presence of a huge, frowning, heavily-armed guard. He indicated by raising his rifle that the door was not for exiting.

I opened my mouth to offer a thin excuse and at that moment there came a commotion at the other end of the room. He was momentarily distracted and moved a few steps from the door. I was through it in a flash, and bolted across the tarmac towards the plane. There was a shout, maybe several, and the next minute I found myself overtaken and surrounded by an assorted rabble of service staff and about five formidable guards. One of them, better dressed than the others, hauled me out of the mob and asked me what I thought I was doing.

'I just wanted a stamp,' I grovelled.

He quietly said to just keep walking, as he pretended to question me. At the plane he sternly recommended that I never do such a thing again. I fled up the steps and collapsed back in my seat in a complete lather. We took off back to Accra a few moments later.

I decided I would happily go back to Freetown but I'd give another visit to Monrovia a miss.

101 Togo

Our next stop was Lome in Togo. The city lies between the Atlantic Ocean and an extensive low-lying wetland, so it's not surprising that we were immediately hit by a damp simmering heat. The city is filled with motorcycles, sand, and buildings of no great consequence. We taxied downtown for the sole purpose of buying our passage out. My energy was sapped by the time we reached the blissful air-conditioning of the Palm Beach Hotel. James disappeared back onto the heaving streets to buy our tickets and, when I'd recovered, I ventured across the road to the beach to take photographs.

Within minutes of setting foot on the sand I was charged by a wave of vendors, moneychangers and souvenir sellers. I beat a cowardly retreat and, breaking through the thinnest ranks, headed for home.

Returning to the hotel at that moment, James caught me hurdling the median barrier, with a dishevelled army in pursuit. I asked him what I looked like.

'Pallid, unathletic and decidedly stressed,' he said.

If Togo were to find oil like its neighbours, it would enjoy more prosperity. As it was, it had little to offer and we were happy enough to fly back to Douala, Cameroon, later in the afternoon to the sanctuary of the Ibis hotel, which was clearly the centre of Douala's lively expatriate life. In the bar a middle-aged African singer was entertaining. Jeans like an undersized cushion cover hugged her voluptuous backside and, released from a red bodice, her cleavage quivered alarmingly when she hit the top notes. The band members looked as if they were searching for earplugs, but no one pushed her off the podium or yelled 'Arrete! Arrete!'

Seeing the expression on our faces the barman leaned across to me. 'She is the manager's "friend",' he said with an extravagant wink.

The next day we went to the airport to see if we could fly to Equatorial Guinea. The outbound Cameroon Airline return flight was full, but by chance there was a Yak 40 on the tarmac which was flying one-way. We figured we could catch that and return on the Air Cameroon flight. We bought tickets and waited. And waited. Two hours went by. The Air Cameroon plane took off. Meanwhile heaps of parcels were being delivered to the ground at the rear of the Yak.

I sidled up to an official. 'What's going on?' I asked.

'The plane has brought the mother of the wife of the president of Equatorial Guinea to go shopping in Douala,' he said. 'When she goes shopping, time means nothing.'

Another half-hour went by. We calculated that there was no way we'd make it to Malabo in time to catch the flight back, cancelled our tickets in a storm of indignity to the amusement of all in the terminal.

CHAPTER TWELVE

central and southern africa

102 Congo

The Cameroon Airlines flight bound for the Congo left the usual one hour late. We landed at Brazzaville and were asked to stay on the plane. A few minutes later we were ordered to disembark and were herded into the transit lounge, which was devoid of furniture except for one broken chair which no one was game to sit on. Through a large open window there was a full view of the tarmac.

An hour passed. We were ordered back on board and settled in for the brief flight to Kinshasa.

'That's ominous – the doors aren't closed,' said James.

The next moment the airport manager appeared. 'Due to a problem encountered on landing, the plane will now go straight back to Douala without passengers,' he announced. 'No bags will be unloaded.'

A riot broke out among the passengers. They mobbed the hapless manager, shouting and waving their arms around like agitated centipedes. He offered an alternative. We could bus to the Congo River and catch the ferry to Kinshasa. The mob was pacified. We debouched and headed for the immigration counter to be issued with visas for the Congo.

Jacques, a nervous Frenchman, hissed to me that there'd been a bird strike and the starboard engine smelled like fried chicken. 'We could have been fried *aussi*,' he said.

We watched the bird-beleaguered plane taxi to the end of the runway, flanked by emergency services. It wound up its engines, turned and came back again. It pulled up outside the terminal. The baggage was off-loaded and then to our great surprise the plane took to the sky. As it became a tiny speck the roomful of people fell quiet. We were stranded in Brazzaville.

The airport manager reappeared, this time with security guards. '*Bonne chance*,' he announced. 'Another plane is arriving soon.'

Jacques piped up that he, for one, was not going to risk another plane ride. He'd rather try his *bonne chance* on the ferry. He left happily waving his visa and we returned yet again to the 'lounge'! Not 30 minutes later the very same plane returned.

103 Democratic Republic of Congo

The flight from Brazzaville to Kinshasa was brief because the two cities are on opposite banks of the Congo River, a breathtaking wide ribbon of grey water that winds through an undulating landscape and breaks into an estuary of swampy channels before pouring itself into the Atlantic.

AN ABSOLUTELY OUTRAGEOUS ADVENTURE

We had planned just to transit through the Aeroport de Maya-Maya in Kinshasa, the capital of this huge country (until recently called Zaire), but to get our bags we had to enter the country and then leave again. In the arrivals hall all eyes seemed to be upon us. A matronly woman wearing a hostess badge approached us, ordered a small ragged baggage man to pick up our luggage and move it, then stuck out her hand for money. The immigration official stamped our passports and instead of returning them, rubbed his stomach and moaned, 'Hungry. I am hungry. Money for food.' 'So are we,' I said, and snatched the passports from his hand. He looked stunned, then waved us away.

From then on it was just a parade of beggars: a mob of taxi drivers outside the terminal wanted money even though we didn't want a taxi. The check-in clerks all asked for money; another hostess approached us with her hand out; the outgoing immigration officer gave us another hungry story. I declined, but with our passports in hand he indicated we should follow him to a side room. Sitting behind a desk was an attractive, uniformed woman who proceeded to grill us for 30 minutes. Taking stock of the armed and scar-faced guards, we settled upon the sum of 500CAF ($US25) and were released.

The Customs officer patted me down with particular attention to my groin and wallet-bearing hip pocket. Then he too asked for money. I slapped his hand from my groin, yelled an expletive and stormed off.

In the departure lounge there was a bar. Behind it was a wall of empty shelves displaying a solitary and empty bottle of beer. I pointed to it. '*Donnez-moi deux, s'il vous plaît*,' I said. Two bottles of beer appeared. The only food in sight was a plate of stale-looking waffles at the end of the counter. '*Deux aussi*,' I said.

The beer, remarkably, was chilled and the waffles were dry and gritty with sand but we ate them because we too were moaning with hunger. We hadn't eaten in 24 hours. The eyes of the two bargirls never left us.

But the best bit and most inventive of extortion in Kinshasa was the toilet experience. An old woman in a filthy apron held a rusting bucket up to me. 'You want water?' she said in French.

'No!'

She looked at me balefully: 'No water, no go.'

'Oh!' I handed her some coins.

She filled her bucket from the tap and poured it down the loo, which still held the malodorous detritus of the last occupant. She put the bucket down and gave me a nod. I was, it appeared, free to pee.

104 Angola

An hour later, at 11 p.m., our flight on a Taag Airlines 737-200 headed south to Luanda in the former Portuguese colony of Angola. The Luanda airport was modern and after Maya-Maya was well-stocked but we had to wait two hours for our bags. By the time our rooms were sorted at the Le Meridien Hotel it was 2 a.m. Apart from the sand-filled waffle at Kinshasa, we still hadn't eaten but it didn't seem worth pursuing. In four hours we would be up again.

In the early light we drove through the town, which is draped over a series of gentle hills, and around a bay that nature has crafted with excellent taste. The buildings confirmed its history of Portuguese occupation and the central palm-lined promenade radiated peace and prosperity.

But out of town on the way to the airport a vast area of slums appeared. Hovels clustered drunkenly around decrepit, half-demolished concrete buildings; sad and aimless people loitered around the pitted roads. Beyond the hills these spreading shantytowns are rapidly multiplying as refugees pour in after Angola's 30-year war, which ended in February 2002.

We had arrived at the airport still without sustenance and as we milled around trying in vain to find something to eat, a tall, coal-black policeman in a crisp blue shirt beckoned to us. He looked like a man of some authority and so we followed him into his office. He stood behind the desk, coughed and then, to our utter astonishment, put out his hand and said 'Kwanza' (money).

'Fucking quanza to you too, mate,' I shouted, turned on my heel and marched out of the office. James followed. He'd gone puce.

After that defiant display we thought it best to get our heads down so we went to the far end of the terminal and wedged ourselves between two large Angolan women who were balancing overstuffed bags on their knees. Only our noses showed. Ten minutes later a dumpy European woman in a Taag uniform came by and prattled something in Portuguese. One of the large women must have seen our blank expressions and translated for us: 'Da women say da time is not right for flying.'

105 Namibia

It was another two hours before we were aloft again, this time crossing the great thirsty expanse of Namibia to land in Windhoek at a small airport with services we hadn't seen for some time. But best of all was a large sign erected on the wall behind the Customs area: 'It is a pleasure and a duty to serve you with a smile. Therefore it is not necessary to tip us.' We stood and stared – we must be in heaven.

Checking in to the reasonably-priced, five-star Kalahari Sands Hotel was like finding an oasis.

I celebrated this return to civilisation by throwing up in the basin the moment I got into my room, struck down by the cold cuts of dodgy-looking meat I'd wolfed down on the Air Angola flight. I emerged just in time to stagger to the airport the next morning.

James, ever more cautious, hadn't eaten the meat, and so he went out on the town. This small Germanic capital between the Atlantic and the Kalahari Desert is in the heart of Namibia, which by all accounts is one of the most fascinating places in Africa – a land of deserts and diamonds, wild animals and wilder coastlines. The city centre is a mixture of modern and German colonial buildings set among lush gardens and tropical flowerbeds.

James enthused over the Cape Dutch-style railway station, the Art Nouveau Lutheran church and, in the middle of Post Street, a pedestrian mall displaying 33 extra-terrestrial boulders weighing 21 tonnes that had plummeted into the desert in 1837. 'I tried five ATMs,' he trumpeted, 'and they all worked.'

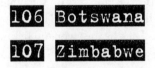

106 Botswana
107 Zimbabwe

It took an effort of will to get myself back to the airport next day. I felt as if a bus had hit me. We were taking a 19-seater Beechcraft to Maun in Botswana and on to Victoria Falls in Zimbabwe. First passengers aboard had to sit up the front to stop the plane tipping back. We were given lunchboxes: inside mine was a bun from which some sort of meat product dangled. I could hardly bear to look at it. We flew over the southern tip of the Okavango swamp where unique wildlife abounds. Unfortunately I couldn't see a thing because there was no window up the front where I was sitting. No matter, I slept. We waited at the small Maun airport for an hour and then flew on for 318 kilometres to Victoria Falls. James said that everywhere he looked there was almost no vegetation. The rains were late, and the drought – on top of Mugabe's brutal policies – was making life here very tough. We could see as soon as we landed that the people were desperate for income, which meant the act of walking anywhere became an exercise in dodging pleas to buy or give money or get them out of the country. Yet they were friendly. How they could keep smiles on their faces was beyond our understanding. Mugabe has sent his nation's economy into free fall, and repression, hyper-inflation and food queues are the people's daily lot.

Neatly cocooned from that reality, we were staying at the Mercure Hotel on the southern bank of the deep, green, sluggish Zambesi River, close to the Victoria Falls. In the morning a troop of vervet monkeys cavorted around in the jungle not far from the balcony on which we were enjoying a good breakfast, my first food in days. The cheekier ones leaped onto the furniture to snatch left-over morsels of food. A guard armed with a slingshot roamed the tables to deal with the intrusion but he mostly missed the monkeys, shattering the crockery on the tables instead.

The sun was well up and a hot wind was already curling around the explosions of foliage by the river and licking at our foreheads as we sipped our second cup of coffee. A monitor lizard wandered through the grass just 10 metres away from us, and a warthog broke from the bushes to trot past with its tail held aloft like a flag bearer.

We took a shuttle to the falls and walked through the forest to get to the viewing platform. A bushbuck tossed its heavy ridged horns and trod delicately across a clearing to hide in the bushes. There were monkeys everywhere, and a corn-coloured meerkat rose up on its hind legs the better to see us. The great river's water level was low, but the tumbling wall of Victoria Falls was still a dramatically impressive sight.

There were few tourists around but a number of Zimbabwean hotel staff caught a ride in the shuttle on their way to their Seventh-Day Adventist church. Lloyd, in a crisp white shirt, was both acting hotel chef and Aids advisor. Alec, a short fellow with a shaved head, told us how in many rural households people have turned to prostitution, theft and eating wild food in order to survive. 'A meat pie in Harare costs the equivalent of $US8.50,' he said. 'Most people cannot pay for food any more. Bakers have been ordered to sell their bread for less than it costs to make it.'

We drove back to the Victoria Falls Airport contemplating that Mugabe would soon be making his own flight for a red-carpet meeting in Paris. There he was to stay with his entourage in an entire wing of the luxurious Hotel Plaza Athenee at a cost of around $NZ40,000 a night.

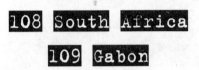

108 South Africa
109 Gabon

Two hours later we were in Johannesburg, South Africa, in a modest hotel room close to the airport. Over the next few days we would be in and out of South Africa quite a few times.

Because we'd missed out the islands of Sao Tome, 440 kilometres off the coast of Gabon, we thought we'd have a refreshing night in Johannesburg and try again by backtracking to Libreville. We'd have to cross Angola and Congo again to get there. James was tearing his hair out trying to find information. There was nothing on the Internet and no Sao Tome Airline offices anywhere. We hoped for better things in Gabon.

When we pitched up at the Johannesburg Airport, I was not in the best frame of mind. A nagging chest infection was still bugging me, I had lost weight from the meat poisoning, and I was tired and frazzled. The incoming plane was late. James speculated as to why. 'I don't care if it's blown up on the bloody runway and taken Libreville with it,' I grumped.

An old Air Gabon 747-200 Combi finally came into view and landed. We boarded to encounter an olfactory assault of old smoke (there was still a smoking section) mingled with stale sweat, food and other accumulated odours of the last 20 years. We had to endure this lingering pong for the four-hour journey north.

Johannesberg - traditional healers' market.

It was 11 p.m. when we arrived at the Novotel, where we had, for a change, booked rooms. The desk attendant, an officious African with an ingratiating smile, looked at us as if we were noxious insects. 'You have no reservations,' he said.

We couldn't be bothered arguing. 'Just give us two rooms,' I said, wanting to block my nose against the fetid air in the lobby.

'You have to pay cash.'

We handed over a wad of Central African francs. He handed over two keys as if they were dead flies. The corridor leading to the rooms smelt of old sweat, beer and mould. The carpet was wrinkled and threadbare. The rooms were disgusting. The white tiles on the floors were awash with water. There were no towels but plenty of cockroaches scuttling around in the corners.

At the reception we'd asked if we could buy bottled water from the bar. *'Non! Fermez,'* our persecutor had said. *'Chambre, chambre,'* he'd waved a dismissive hand towards the stairs. There was no sign of any drinking water in the *chambre* either. That was the last straw. We picked up our bags, marched downstairs and demanded our money back.

'No, I cannot give it to you.'

I ordered a taxi, gave him one of my impressive thunderous looks and we marched from the shabby foyer. As we got into the taxi one of the security guards came up to the window and asked for money.

'Fuck off,' I spat and slammed the door.

We were transported to another part of town and checked into the Intercontinental for the night, which while not perfect, was far superior.

This appalling hotel encounter in Libreville was something of a surprise. The former French colony of Gabon is not quite as wealthy as it was when oil, uranium and manganese discoveries heralded a heady 10 years of prosperity. But we'd been told that it had ocean-view hotels of good standard, a high-rise business centre and fancy shops, and that the people had a sophisticated night-life and drank lots of French champagne.

The next morning James took a taxi to town and stopped on the way at the Novotel on the way to demand our money back.

'It's an old dog in the daylight,' he reported. 'I walked to the reception desk and announced myself in a tone that expected a fight. The dumpy woman behind the desk pulled a face as if she had just trodden in something disgusting and referred to a small dapper fellow in a suit who dispatched another lackey to fetch a brown envelope. Inside was our cash, which was handed over without a word.'

James then drove on to the city to find information about Sao Tome, but no one spoke English and he made no headway. He booked return tickets to Malabo in Equatorial Guinea. This time we hoped the shopping antics of the mother of the wife of the president weren't going to stop us.

110 Equatorial Guinea

We flew the distance in the oldest 737-200 James or I had ever seen and we gave Air Gabon the crappiest aircraft award, heading off Air Ivoire. Much of the inside lining was missing, seats wouldn't come upright, the carpet was corrugated and worn, the last passengers' food wrapped in plastic was stuffed down beside the fuselage and the air, once again, smelled vile.

The five formerly Spanish islands of Equatorial Guinea lie in the Gulf of Guinea. The country also includes the small mainland area of Rio Muni that lies between Cameroon and Gabon. We flew over the island of Bioko, which looked craggy and volcanic and was covered in dense forest and rimmed by decent beaches, and then landed at Malabo.

The airport was being reconstructed, probably with funds from the recently discovered oil reserves here. A VIP building had been started and looked as if it would be rather splendid. But now we had to park ourselves in a temporary and airless shack.

Since the country's independence in 1968 it has been dogged, like so many in Africa, by despotic rulers, corruption and mismanagement. But things are rapidly improving. Malabo had a strong Spanish flavour and was said to be a compact, attractive, tourist-friendly place which was being polished up with oil money. During the worst times many of the citizens fled as refugees to neighbouring countries. We did our own fleeing on the same plane we'd come in on an hour before.

There followed another night in Libreville. Tomorrow would be my 45th birthday but I wasn't in the mood to acknowledge it, and deferred any form of celebration until we were back in South Africa.

Next day we at last found the Air Sao Tome office, and learned that a flight was going out to the islands that night but it was full. The next available flight was in three days, but both the return

162

flight and the island's limited accommodation were booked out.

And so my birthday marked not only my approaching middle age but also the most critical moment of the Quest. If we didn't go to Sao Tome, we wouldn't be going to every nation in the world. If we did go to Sao Tome, the rest of our scheduling would be thrown into a chaos we might not be able to resolve.

I thought about it long and hard and then announced, 'Let's forget it.'

James felt like giving up the whole ridiculous scheme and going home. I felt annoyed at myself for not thinking more laterally. We just had to get over it.

To take my mind off it, I went to every Internet café in town to try to pick up email from my family, who surely wouldn't have forgotten my birthday. No contact was possible. I went back to my hotel and ordered room service.

'What is the *soup de jour*?' I asked.

'The soup of the day, sir.'

'No, no. What is the soup of the day?'

'It's the *soup de jour*, sir.'

I went to bed after a plate of soup-with-no-name, a tired, dejected man wondering what the hell he was doing.

It was with relief that we flew back to Johannesburg and the Airport Intercontinental Hotel next day to take a few days off. We celebrated my birthday with a fine dinner and two bottles of wine and braced ourselves for the tasks ahead.

I remember Johannesburg for its mountainous piles of gold-mine tailings; the FNB Stadium where throngs of Cup Final soccer supporters were pushing and shoving and waving their colourful flags; the Aids awareness posters everywhere; and the 16-storey, glass De Beers offices built in the shape of a diamond. We also went to see the humble building in Fox Street where, in 1962, Nelson Mandela had hidden from the police in his lawyer's office. It is derelict now, its second level boarded up and the ground floor blackened by fire.

We drove through Soweto with its myriad matchbox houses and through the once well-ordered streets of Johannesburg, where a jumble of vendors crowded the pavements and barbers shaved peppercorn hair under canvas awnings. But the highlight was the Traditional Healers' Market set up under a motorway over-bridge and stretching for about a kilometre. It was a noisy colourful place that sold an extraordinary collection of potions, herbs, roots and animal skins, parts and bones.

111 Swaziland

On 1 December we left for Swaziland on a tiny BA Jetstream 41. Southern Africa, like many other parts of the continent, was desperate for rain. The red soil of the countryside was covered by a thin green film of cultivation. But flying east we had to dodge three huge banks of black cumulus clouds spitting lightning. Maybe the rains had come.

Swaziland is the smallest country in the Southern Hemisphere, a kingdom where King Mswati III's omnipotence was currently being challenged by strong unions. Opposition parties were still illegal. The local paper reported the Prime Minister's chastisement of two Court of Appeal judges for questioning a royal decree which, he'd said, 'is not to be challenged and is neither debatable nor negotiable'.

King Mswati recently bought a private plane costing millions of dollars, while many of his loyal subjects were in desperate need of food. A plane, explained the king, would enable him to go to Europe and the USA to enlist more aid money.

We descended to the capital, Manzini, where an official greeted us with a placard bearing our names and hurried us through immigration procedures so we could catch the flight back again.

CHAPTER THIRTEEN

East Africa

112 Lesotho

We returned to South Africa and the next morning departed for
Lesotho stuffed once again into the tiny seats of a South African
Airways Express twin turbo-prop aircraft. On its way north the
plane dodged another huge storm and I hoped the people below
were celebrating. We looked down on the open spaces of this tiny
land-locked nation – one of the world's smallest – which is
barricaded from South Africa by high mountains.

As in Swaziland, our brief 40-minute stay at the airport at
Maseru offered no more than a glimpse of life at ground level.
Like Swaziland, Lesotho is a kingdom, but King Letsie III's rule
is not absolute as the country also has a democratic congress.

The recent closure of mines in Zimbabwe has resulted in large
numbers of Lesotho's young men returning unemployed and

often HIV/AIDs infected. One quarter of the population of Lesotho now has the disease.

We returned to South Africa yet again.

113 Mozambique

In Mozambique we were visiting Quelimane, where the Save the Children Fund was running an Aids education programme. Mozambique had been hit hard, not only by Aids but also by a brutal, protracted civil war. The countryside is littered with undetonated land mines and other dangerous debris.

We landed at the capital Maputo in the south, which was once heralded for the beauty of its Portuguese-inspired architecture. Twenty years of war had left it scarred and broken but in the last few years it had slowly begun to be rebuilt. Aged, clattering taxis prowled the streets past refurbished and well-stocked shops filled with big-brand clothing, computer and electronic outlets that were appearing along the run-down boulevards.

When we flew north via Tete to Quelimane, Mozambique's fourth-largest city, the country below us looked weary, under-populated and splinter-dry. Clusters of mud-and-thatch rondavels were scattered across the landscape but few larger towns.

At the small airport a slender woman in a green cotton dress and sandals approached us.

'You must be John and James,' she said, extending a slim hand. Sally Griffen was from England and was living in Mozambique as the HIV advisor for Save the Children. She directed us to her Landcruiser and in 15 minutes we pulled up in front of Tim Barker's whitewashed bungalow.

Tim was an affable Englishman about 28 years of age who sported a thin moustache and smoked roll-your-owns wrapped in dark liquorice paper. He was the Save the Children's programme director and had worked for the last 10 years in places like Sudan and Croatia. We left our gear at his house and drove on to the Save the Children office to meet the other workers, Etelvina da Cunha and Albertina Muchanga from Mozambique and Carlos Barros, a visiting researcher.

The programme is run in a village in the Namuinho barrio nearby. 'It can take a year just to get people facing up to Aids,' Sally said. 'To get them to understand and prevent infection, we have to dispel the myths that exist: that Aids is transmitted by mosquitoes; that an HIV-positive person can contaminate the water, which normally comes from a central well; that sex with a virgin is curative; or that condoms are responsible.

'Often Aids is initially contracted by people who are educated or well-off because they have the opportunity to travel out of the village. Away from home they have sexual adventures, which is where the trouble starts. Truckies catch the disease by liaisons with roadside sex workers.'

At the office we read some of the horrendous statistics. In Mozambique alone there were 1.2 million orphans, most of them due to Aids; that's one in every six children. One out of eight people in the country was HIV-positive. The disease had already orphaned more than 11 million children in Africa, and had affected many more.

'The care-giving role for orphaned children,' Sally said, 'is often thrust upon ageing aunts and uncles or, in many cases, the oldest child. While we try to give essential assistance to those who are dying and to orphans, the only real hope is education. But it's a long process. Thousands of counsellors have to be trained and then sent to villages. Disseminating information through the school system won't work because at the end of the civil war in 1991 there were only six secondary schools operating in the country – 600 have been rebuilt in the last 10 years but there needs to be 6000.'

We piled into the Landcruiser again and drove through

extensive coconut plantations to the village in Namuinho, where we pulled up outside a tin-roofed shelter around which crowded 50 villagers. Fifteen healthy-looking adolescents dressed in white T-Shirts were sitting on coconut matting in the shelter. They had been rehearsing a play for our arrival, which prompted the local TV station to send out a camera crew. Contained in the African al fresco theatre was a simple message: a boy had contracted HIV/Aids and went to a witch doctor for help. The witch doctor said, 'No, you must go to the hospital to get treated there. I cannot help.'

I took a photograph of one of the performers, a 16-year-old girl called Filomena Goveia, and I asked her what her dream was. She looked at me shyly. 'I would like to go on at school,' she said. 'But I am afraid because to get a place I might have to have sex with one of the teachers.' Teachers have been accused of getting young girls to exchange sexual favours for a place in school or even good marks.

Dinner that night followed drinks under the gazebo in Tim's back yard and then with Tim, Sally and Carlos we went to an Italian restaurant said to be the best in town. The food was mediocre but the company was excellent. Also there was Patrick Craddock who made health videos, and his wife who ran an Internet publishing company.

'Getting health messages to people isn't easy,' Patrick said. 'Once teachers are trained they have to be physically transported to the villages and many roads are all but destroyed. Horses and donkeys that might have helped were wiped out in the war and the only way of getting around is by walking or, where there are roads, by clapped-out bicycle if you happen to have one.

'Out of every 100 households, 38 have a radio and less than four a TV, and the official literacy rate while at 40 percent is really only 20 percent, even less in rural areas. It's not hopeless, just really slow.'

We slept at Tim's house that night and the next morning went to the local hospital – a three-roomed basic building, cooled by two large ceiling fans, where Aids testing was for the moment free. Two barefoot men were waiting to give blood samples, looking as if they were about to be executed. They looked healthy enough, but Albertina said that looks were deceiving.

According to a world study HIV/Aids is not so easily transmissible in healthy populations, but in sub-Saharan Africa people are not healthy. Many have parasites, malnutrition, malaria, cholera and poor immune systems, so the chances of contracting it are high.

We left the two men to their fate and went to lunch, this time at a Cuban restaurant on the side of a main street. We ate tough steak rolls and paused between mouthfuls to deal with beggars, staring kids, and walking department-store vendors who were selling anything from toilet brushes to CDs, plastic raincoats (there had been no rain for months), buckets and combs. I didn't see any condoms.

Down the road a bit I photographed a little girl of about eight who said her name was Lanomo. Her dream was poignant: 'I would like to have food, like you,' she said.

Later that day, on the return flight to Maputo, we sat next to Renardo Ferbero, a Portuguese Angolan who'd recently moved to Mozambique from South Africa and bought 2000 hectares of farmland that carried 20 sheep or one cow to the hectare. James asked him if he used sheep dogs. 'No,' he said, 'just the natives. It's cheaper.'

I hid my disgust with a lop-sided smile. We flew on and spent the night back in South Africa.

On the morning of 4 December we flew from Johannesburg to Reunion Island, 3047 kilometres away off the east coast, pausing for three hours on the island of Mauritius. One seat on an earlier flight was on offer and I accepted it, leaving James looking rather irritable in the departure lounge, but pleased to see the back of me.

I landed at Roland Garros airport 11 kilometres east of the capital of St Denis. French holidaymakers are attracted to this speck in the Indian Ocean where untamed mountains are wrapped in spectacular tropical forests and high-rises and resort hotels cascade down the sides of the mountains to the sea. The culture here was French Creole but also strongly Roman Catholic judging by the string of little shrines along the road into the town.

I was driven into the hills to our hotel by a driver with grey hair sprouting wildly from under a colourful cap and a pinched fox-like face. I doubt he worked out that I didn't speak French because he didn't stop talking long enough for me to get a word in.

We were staying at the Mercure Oreolia, which looked over a distant beach to the sea. It was a bit like being in a spruced-up Nice.

114 Comoros

Next day's long flight was west to the islands of Comoros, between Mozambique and Madagascar, and back. The sapphire-blue sea was studded with islands that shimmered like jewels and was everything that we had expected to see in the Caribbean but didn't. A shining blue sky melted into the blue horizon.

Most of the time we flew over the Indian Ocean except for a brief stop on the tiny island of Petite Terre, in the group of islands known as Mayotte, which was a flawless arrangement of forests and high peaks.

The Federal Islamic Republic of the Comoros – a big name for a small place – was 240 kilometres to the north. It is also referred to as the Coup Coup Islands because it has had so many riots there over the years. We landed at Hahaya Airport on Grand Comore near the town of Moroni. Unlike Mayotte, the volcanic Comoros islands were barren.

Perhaps the archipelago's greatest claim to fame is that in 1938 the coelacanth, a fossil fish thought to have been extinct for 70 million years, was discovered alive here. A visiting museum curator spotted one in the bottom of a fisherman's basket. The locals had been catching them and frying them up for dinner for years.

The immigration officers were more curious about our New Zealand passports than the coelacanth. They held it under the 'black light' to reveal the security markings which they thought were *magnifique* and *formidable* for the simple reason that the light revealed kiwis, ferns and a map of New Zealand.

115 Madagascar

An hour later we were flying back along the route we had come, landing at Mayotte, Reunion and eventually back to Antananarivo in the island of Madagascar, which we'd already flown over three times. Our overnight visit, however, did not start well. After an excruciatingly long time in the immigration queue, a short, self-important fellow with large round glasses tapped James on the shoulder and indicated, 'Come with me.' He took him to a cubicle and patted him down, felt his wallet and made him produce it. James opened it and the man saw the $US100 he had inside. 'I want money,' he said.

'There was no way he was going to get a hundred US dollars,' said James later, 'but he wasn't the sort of guy I thought I'd like to trifle with. I rummaged through my wallet and found 100 Mauritian rupees, which is about $US4. "You change," I said thrusting them at him. The official gave me a smug smile, pocketed the money and pulled the curtain of the cubicle back to let me go.'

We pushed our way through a trumpeting crowd of taxi drivers and moneychangers who followed us outside the terminal like a swarm of bees. It was night, pitch-black and raining hard, and in seconds we were sodden.

We picked one taxi driver. I put my arm around his shoulders and told the rest of them to 'bugger off'. The chosen one was as black as the night, a short slender man with prominent teeth. We rumbled off down the road and it became apparent from the way we sashayed around the corners that the vehicle's brakes were far from adequate. One windscreen wiper worked, one didn't, and the headlights were out of action. Parking lights lit our path dimly and only a stab of forked lightning every now and then told us we were still on the road.

The driver kept leaning forward to rub at the inside of the window with his sleeve in the vain hope this might improve his vision. It was a drive we won't forget in a hurry, and the stray dog he swiped as we swung crazily around a corner probably won't forget it either.

But things improved. The Ibis Hotel's staff greeted us with the sort of enthusiasm accorded to rock stars and dawn brought hot fine weather. We walked downhill from the hotel to Independence Boulevard lined by colourful, ornate buildings that looked like many of the historical ones of France. Alongside a cluttered make-shift market, people scavenged through a ditch full of rubbish. For most Madagascans life is far from caviare and champagne.

Elections had just been held in Madagascar: Marc Ravalomanana, who had deposed the dictatorial President Ratsiraka the year before, was elected to legitimate presidency by a large majority. From that point political and economic stability was expected to improve. It certainly needed to. But people seemed cheerful enough and, apart from at the airport, we were not pestered for money.

Madagascar is the fourth-largest island in the world and known for its odd wildlife. It has 28 unique species of lemur, half the world's species of chameleon, 1000 endemic orchids and unique cacti and aloes. Sadly, slash-and-burn agricultural techniques over the centuries had destroyed all but 15 percent of the rainforest, and soil erosion is a big problem. Soil exposure has resulted in Madagascar being dubbed Red Island.

116 Mauritius

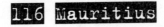

In the late afternoon, when we departed for Mauritius again, the airport was chaotic, with close to 300 people shoving to reach the check-in counters through one small gap. We stood back trying to work out the best way of getting through.

Slightly to the side of the mob of bobbing black heads was a tall European woman who seemed to be making some forward progress. Without hesitation we hitched ourselves to her side. The crowd parted and we were ushered through.

Paying pays off in Africa. She had, it transpired, paid a backhander to the security guards and because we were the only other white faces in the airport it was assumed we were travelling with her. That is how we met Doctor Monica Nolan, an ebullient, auburn-haired young woman from Australia.

Mauritius is 800 kilometres to the east of Madagascar and, as we descended over the lush-looking island and landed at Sir Seewoosagur Ramgoolam international airport near Mahebourg in the southeast, I was reminded of Fiji.

We taxied to the Southern Pacific Hotel and waited for an hour while staff consulted and rustled through their booking sheets, eventually to pronounce that there was no room at the inn. With Monica in tow we took another taxi to the other side of the island only 58 kilometres away where, at the Emeraud Hotel at Belle Mer, there was more than adequate accommodation. The manager must have thought we had lascivious intentions towards our female companion because, in that sprawling complex, she gave us three rooms as far apart as possible.

Lascivious intent was far from our minds but it is fair to say that Monica's company at dinner made our night. She knew Africa well and had just been ordered out of Abidjan in Cote D'Ivoire, where she had been in charge of an Aids research programme, because of that country's gathering civil war. She was taking a holiday before heading home to Australia to await reassignment.

Dinner was hot lamb curry. Mauritius is more Indian than African and the dominant religion is Hindu, but British and French occupations have also left their mark. The island has many pampering beach resorts that pander to rich sun-seekers from Europe. There are many more people than indigenous animals now, but the island's most famous was the dodo.

117 Seychelles

Morning saw us on an Air Seychelles flight north to Victoria on Mahe Island in the Seychelles. This tiny airline proudly owned only two aircraft. The one we were on was a brand-new 737-300. The chicken served at lunch was excellent, the music soothingly classical, the crew good-humoured and the view magnificent. Looking down on the island of Mahe we saw dramatic thickly forested peaks and hills tumbling down to a flat plain that stretched to the edge of the sea.

Our visit was brief. At the down-at-heel airport I made a beeline for the air-conditioned departure lounge to get away from the insufferable heat and await our British Airways flight to Nairobi. James wanted to see more. The Seychelles comprises 115 islands and atolls which are havens for a profusion of birds and tropical reef fish and only 80,000 people – a mix of Indians, Arabs, Africans and mainly French Europeans. He stood gazing at the trees across the tarmac, dreaming of the life in the wild.

I read in the inflight magazine that the female nut of the coco-de-mer tree was the symbol of the island. There are claims that it, not the apple, was the biblical forbidden fruit. If so, it seemed an extraordinary choice for it was not a fruit of any beauty, resembling, in fact, a giant, hairy scrotum.

 118 Kenya

We flew on to Kenya and landed at Jomo Kenyatta Airport. On the way into Nairobi, menacing-looking police armed with automatic rifles were stationed every hundred metres or so. They stood on overhead bridges and blocked all side roads along the way. The atmosphere was tense. Elections were in progress: the reigning president had come in on a flight just after ours and would soon be following us into town. But that wasn't the only reason for the jitters. The country was still reeling from the bombing of the Mombasa Hotel a few days before; two days before that missiles had narrowly missed an Israeli airliner taking off; and there was compelling evidence that terrorist cells were operating in the area.

The Hilton Nairobi hotel had also had a bomb scare the day before our arrival, which we learned only after we'd checked in. The bags of every guest were searched and guards, rigid with suspicion, prowled the corridors. We slept peacefully, too tired to do anything else.

Nairobi was to be the base for our sorties into Zambia, Malawi, Tanzania, Sudan, Eritrea and Ethiopia. James discovered next morning that all our bookings for flights to those countries had been cancelled, which saw him in town at sparrow-up in the morning to reorganise the schedule.

The centre of town with its smart offices and hotels was cosmopolitan with facilities which you couldn't find in the rest of Africa. James saw only one beggar – a young woman with two children who were sitting out on the pavement in the rain – but there were plenty of prostitutes, hawkers and layabouts. He also became entangled in a noisy demonstration which surged down River Road and was certainly something to do with the elections.

But behind this sophisticated centre are sobering slums. Caroline Kabena, the head receptionist at the hotel, took us to her home in Githurai on the northern outskirts of the city so that we could visit her mother and take pictures of her two young brothers. She'd hired a taxi driven by a tall lanky African with a name that sounded like Maninchonpopo. We called him Manchester United which was easier to say and hugely pleased him.

Off the main drag the roads were appalling. Manchester United was forced to move at snail's pace and in many places we had to get out and walk behind the car so it could clear the rutted mud tracks. It was reminiscent of Haiti. The houses were just small, square, concrete dwellings with tin roofs. There was one power line in the village but little sign of electrical appliances or lights.

Manchester United also managed to sever some of the area's water supply when he drove over a boulder which had been positioned in an open area to protect the village water main. With water gushing behind us we left him to the mercy of the angry residents who had gathered around to remonstrate, and walked the rest of the way to Caroline's family home.

Caroline was a slim, smartly dressed, well-educated young woman and so the bare-basics home she came from surprised us. Outside it was a yard of rubble and grass. The house itself was built of concrete block and comprised three tiny rooms, a small sitting room and a kitchen the size of a wardrobe. A single tap in the kitchen was the only sign of plumbing and the few pieces of furniture were clean but very old. Here Caroline had lived with her brothers and mother. How they all managed to sleep in the space was a mystery.

Their mother was thrilled that her sons were the chosen ones, and ushered us into her humble dwelling and offered us tea and bananas. The boys had been scrubbed up and dressed in their best for the occasion. One of the abiding images I have of Nairobi is Mother Kabena's proud smile as she brushed a speck of dirt off her son's carefully ironed T-shirt and directed him to stand in front of the camera, with a gaggle of children from the village giggling and whispering as they watched from behind the fence.

119 Zambia

It was 8 December when we flew to Lusaka in Zambia. We had only 50 minutes at the airport before catching an onward flight to Blantyre. The transfer was doomed from the start. The tarmac bus took us to the far end of the airport and we had to get ourselves back to the service area. We queued in the incredibly slow transit queue and, when we started appealing for help to get through in time, a nasty little man in a grey suit came mincing over, snatched the tickets off us and disappeared.

By the last boarding call for our flight we were bleating. Then a short, plump, comfortable-looking African woman approached us, with a smile that revealed her good nature. She turned out to be a disguised angel. 'What are you doing here?' she asked. We explained the situation. She turned on her heel, marched off in the same direction that grey-suit had disappeared, and a few minutes later reappeared with him in tow still clutching our tickets. She grabbed the tickets off him. He tried in vain to grab them back. Then our angel grasped us by an arm apiece and propelled us through immigration, nodded at the startled officers, shoved us through the departure lounge and almost threw us through the doors in the direction of our plane. 'You go,' she said. 'I'll sort him out.'

I've no doubt that she did. We ran to the plane shouting our love and gratitude.

120 Malawi

And so we flew on to Malawi, looking down on vast reaches of forest which James found encouraging after the naked state of much of Africa. There was intensive cropping on the flats around the city and in the distance the rippling extent of Lake Malawi, which comprises one fifth of the country's area.

After the Lusaka episode we disembarked at Chileka Airport in Blantyre feeling a little apprehensive. But here we were met by the most robustly cheerful people we'd found anywhere in Africa. It started as we passed through immigration and continued with everyone we met. A smiling clerk re-ticketed several days of onward travel. On the wall behind him was a picture of the president.

'What do you think of Bakili Muluzi?' I asked him.

'Not good and not bad,' he said.

In the lounge I talked to the steward, a dapper Malawian with a deep voice, perfect diction and a colourful command of the English language. His name was Belton Zale.

'Malawi is lucky,' he said, because the government has been relatively stable. After independence Dr Hastings Banda was the president for 30 years. He was removed in 1994 when he was accused of masterminding the assassination of members of the opposition party. Most of the infrastructure that the British built is still here. Schooling is free up until form one and the literacy rate is 60 percent, which is high for Africa.

'Unfortunately 800,000 refugees fled Mozambique during the troubles there. They settled here and that has put pressure on the economy. We also have a drought and food is getting scarce.

'But I'm happy,' he beamed. 'I could be living in Mauritania.'

When he wandered off we ran the taxi test to see if other Malawians were as pleasant. Outside the terminal we pretended to order a taxi. No one mobbed us or bombarded us with African-style sales patter. One man from the front of the taxi queue came forward. His smile was a sparkling wreath of goodwill.

'Can I help you, sir?' he said, in the Queen's English.

'I really wish you could,' I said, 'but unfortunately I have a plane to catch.'

'Well, I hope you come back, sir.'

'I certainly will.'

121 Tanzania

With a degree of reluctance we flew northeast to Dar es Salaam. Coming from the higher and cooler altitude of Blantyre, it was a shock to step into the steamy heat of the African coast again.

Ephim, the Swahili taxi driver who took us to our hotel, was determined to give us his views on the city and the state of the nation. His main beef was about the large Indian population in Tanzania, which for years had been the backbone of small trade but had also, he said, ripped off local Africans by charging them on a different scale from anybody else and making them pay for things like paper bags.

'They don't pay taxes and they send their profits out of the country,' he said. 'We have taken things into our own hands.' His eyes rolled with satisfaction. 'We do not do business with Indians unless we have to. It's better to deal with South African businesses. Electricity, roading and water management are all being managed by South African companies now.'

To get to our hotel, the Golden Tulip, we drove past the harbour crammed with an incongruous mix of Arab dhows and ocean liners. Dar es Salaam means 'safe port' in Swahili. And for a long time it was – under the steely socialist hand of President Julius Nyerere who ruled for 24 years after the German then British occupations. He retired in 1985.

'As a socialist nation the Americans didn't like us,' said Ephim. 'Nyerere was backed by the Chinese, who helped build the country's infrastructure.'

Secure in my room that night I did some calculations. We had been on the road for 105 days. We had taken 154 flights on 68 different airlines, and had been to 121 nations.

122 Uganda

We flew back to Nairobi next day and in the evening took a one-hour flight to Entebbe in Uganda and back, on Kenyan Airways. Approaching Entebbe we had a marvellous view of Lake Victoria, the source of the Nile, which stretches out like a great, grey-blue, shimmering plain. Even at full altitude we couldn't see the other end of it 320 kilometres away to the south.

On the ground Timothy Kintu Magambo, an airport official, politely spirited us from the arrivals hall to the departure area. I took a photograph of him, a tall, smiling, athletic man who moved with the fluid grace of a gazelle. He shook his head in disbelief when we told him we were only staying for half an hour. We didn't tell him that tomorrow we'd be flying to Sudan, Eritrea, Ethiopia and back to Nairobi.

CHAPTER FOURTEEN

Northeast Africa

123 Sudan
124 Eritrea

The first sector was to Khartoum in Sudan. We flew over the dun-brown stretches of Northern Kenya past the bright turquoise Lake Turkana, the world's largest desert lake, clipped a corner of the Sudd – the enormous swamp the size of Wales that formed such an impassable barrier to European explorers a hundred or so years ago – and finally flew along the course of the White Nile. The water was opaque reflecting the morning. At its confluence with the Blue Nile that flows from Ethiopia, we looked down on the dusty spread of Khartoum, a large sprawling tangle of buildings on either side of the shadowy banks of the rivers. As we landed we could also see the jumbled bodies of about 40 discarded aeroplanes in a tangled pile at one side of the runway.

From there we flew east and an hour later arrived at Asmara in Eritrea, which is on an extensive plateau 2350 metres above sea level. As our plane came to a halt on the tarmac, a lumbering grey US Starlifter was taxiing down the runway, leaving behind a massive stretch of red carpet – alas not for us. Heavily-armed UN peacekeepers were everywhere. They eyed us suspiciously as we walked from the tarmac to the terminal. We later learned they were ensuring that US Secretary of Defence Donald Rumsfeld left Asmara in one piece. He had been meeting with local officials, no doubt discussing how the US presence might be beefed up in the region for the forthcoming attack on Iraq.

We passed the hour in Eritrea talking to an upstanding 50-year-old Eritrean in a Western suit who was the manager of airport services for Eritrean Airlines. Fekadu Kahsay had survived Eritrea's 30-year-long struggle with Ethiopia which had only ended that year: 70,000 of his countrymen did not survive and 100,000 others had been left maimed or disabled.

'There has been more trouble,' he said. 'Although the troubles were settled by the Hague Convention there's still tension on the border. That's why there are so many UN troops. Thousands of land mines litter the countryside. But Asmara is a very safe city. I am sorry you will not see it. There are many fine Italian Art Deco buildings and a wonderful cathedral.'

One of our fellow passengers flying into Asmara had been Jack Barker, a paunchy, red-haired Englishman. He was there to ride from Asmara down to the Red Sea on the bicycle which he unfolded from his baggage. He assured us it was all downhill, or at least he hoped it was. As we took to the air again, I looked down on the rugged road stretching way down to the coast, and I hoped so too.

We flew back to Nairobi. With all this travelling my fuse was getting short. Much to the astonishment of the immigration officer, I flew into a rage when he pointed out that our visas had expired even though we'd paid for them only the night before. My language was not that of an English gentleman. A white South African, built like a Springbok prop, lumbered over to me, planted a calloused hand on my neck and hauled me away. 'Calm down, son,' he said. 'You don't understand what can happen to you here.'

In a fatherly fashion, he ordered me to go and see the immigration chief, a middle-aged African woman who might have been good-looking if she hadn't had such a scowl on her face.

'You have a choice,' she said, looking at me as if I'd just stamped on her toe. 'You spend the night in the transit lounge or you apologise to the official.'

'Exactly what I was planning to do,' I grovelled. I went over to the chap I'd bawled at. He was much shorter than me, a cheerful-looking man in a black suit. 'I am really sorry,' I said. 'I am ashamed. I need a cigarette and I've had a long, tiring day.'

He grinned. 'Don't worry. I work for the government. People always shout at me.' He was a man of generous spirit.

I was allowed to buy a visa but the sour atmosphere I'd created around me remained. That night, alone in my room at the hotel, I sat in bed and remonstrated with myself for acting so appallingly. I felt unnerved and enfeebled by my own outburst. This was the lowest point of the trip. I really wondered what the hell I was doing here in this place, unplugged from my own world.

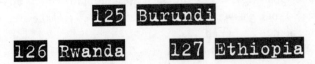

125 Burundi

126 Rwanda   127 Ethiopia

I kept my head down when I went to the airport next morning. We were off to Burundi's capital Bujumbura, which lies in the shadow of Congo's high escarpment at the head of Lake Tanganyika. On the way into the town I noticed a slim barefoot boy balancing a huge load of around 50 bananas on his head. His worn T-shirt was too big for him. His jeans were patched and tattered, his dark skin engrained with dust. I ordered the taxi to halt and climbed out with my camera.

'*Bonjour. Comment appellez-vous?*' I said.

'*Je m'appelle Havyaramama Desmire,*' he said shyly.

Our taxi driver interpreted his story. Havyaramama was 16 and had been the breadwinner for his family since he was 11. His father died when he was a baby and his mother, who continued to live in his village 100 km to the north, sent him to live with a fruit wholesaler in Bujumbura. His keep was taken out of his pay, which left him with $US3 at the end of each month. He sent this to his mother to help care for his three brothers.

Photo taken, we took him up the road in the taxi so that he would not be torn apart by the crowd that had gathered around us and handed him what was the equivalent of two months' pay for him, two glasses of beer for us. He looked uncertain as if he knew there would be some unpleasant task attached to the money. The driver explained that it was a gift. As we climbed back into the taxi he stood there stunned with the enormity of what had just happened. I looked back through the grimy window as we drove off and a smile was spreading like sunshine across his face.

The deeply divided social order in Burundi between the tall lean Tutsi of the north and the small stocky Hutu of the south had led to appalling violence and the massacres of thousands on both sides. When we were there, a peace accord to end the civil war was about to be signed.

War had ravaged the city centre. The shops were boarded up, the dusty roads scoured and gouged, skinny dogs and listless kids in rags stared at us but kept their distance. The women still wore their colourful cascading gowns and turbans but no other adornment.

We wandered through a very large open-sided market under iron roofs. It was abuzz with people sifting through the piles of fruit, eggs, mealy-meal, crude utensils and plastic bags. Our driver said that most of the fighting had taken place in the forested hills that surrounded the city. He drove us to the top of a prominent bluff beyond Bujumbura, a suburb for the well-to-do, and pointed out the war zones and Lake Tanganyika, which though 25 kilometres wide was dwarfed by the hazy, looming mountains of the Congo.

We returned to the airport to find that our reservations on the next flight had been cancelled. 'But,' said the besuited station-master, looking very pleased with himself, 'I managed to rebook you, suh.' Actually, and as per normal, the plane was only half-full.

It was a soft, black-velvet night when we touched down in Rwanda for a short transit stop. We got off the plane, touched the tarmac, looked at the stars and then climbed back on board again to fly to Ethiopia.

We were driving to our hotel just before midnight. Stars still sparkled down at us and the city flickered and swam with lights. I was looking forward to two days' rest here in Addis Ababa – but adjoining the Hilton Hotel where we were staying was a large mosque. Emanating from it through the night was what seemed to be a continual call to prayer which sounded like a herd of lost cows. The next night the calls were less frequent but they irked the neighborhood's dog population, which then filled in the gaps with their own mournful howling. Deprived of a decent sleep, I spent much of the two days in my room trying to throw off a cloak of desolation and catching up on the web diary. This constant need to file reports was consuming what little free time we had.

James organised our flight to Riyadh in Saudi Arabia in the morning and met me for lunch before we were to depart for the airport. When he returned to his room there was a note under his door informing him that the Saudis could not let us into the country without a transit visa and of course by this time the visa office was closed for the day.

128 Djibouti

So next day, because we hadn't gone to Saudi, we found ourselves on a Fokker 50 flying to Djibouti. We intended to drive from there to Somalia and back, and then fly on to Yemen that same night. Because we had no visa for Somalia either, we'd have to wing it.

The US military build-up at the Special Forces Base which adjoins the Djibouti airport was awe-inspiring and not a little unnerving. The colossal area, enclosed by a high dirt wall, was patrolled by heavily armed Hummer vehicles protecting the rows and rows of permanent hangars. There were about 30 jet fighters in huge concrete bunkers and military personnel were everywhere. The United States had issued 'don't visit' warnings for Djibouti, which probably meant that it didn't want too much said about these activities.

During Iraq's invasion of Kuwait in 1990, President Hassan Gouled of Djibouti played a double hand. He gave lip service to opposing the military build-up against Iraq while he allowed France to increase its military forces. The current president, Ismael Omar Guelleh, strengthened the country's ties to France and allowed a build-up of French soldiers. Clearly he was allowing the Americans in as well.

At the airport we were enthusiastically welcomed by a big-hearted, fair-haired Kiwi called Paula whom we'd met on the Internet. She was working as a logistic supplier for a contractor to the US Army. She hugged us as if we were long-lost friends, then handed us a bagful of New Zealand treats such as Peanut Slabs and Raro. As well, there was everything we would need for the trip to Somalia — water, fruit and local currency. 'I have arranged for two men from a major hardware wholesaler here to take you in one of their vehicles which is making a scheduled delivery to the Somalia border town of Lowracado,' she said.

We'd worried about getting to Somalia for a long time and this wonderful woman had solved everything.

Paula introduced us to Faysal, who spoke a little English, and Idres, both tall blue-black Djiboutians who appeared very laid-back about the adventure. They had no doubt done it many times before.

The 45 kilometres trip to the border with Ethiopa and Somalia started where the US army base finished. On either side of the road spread the city dump, a kilometre-long jumble stacked with rusting cars, machine corpses, discarded cans and assorted garbage. In amongst this was a second-hand market of hopeful vendors milling around crude notices advertising items deemed to be of value.

The asphalt then turned into grey-brown sand and for the next 35 kilometres the vehicle picked its way across a corrugated, stone-strewn goat track through the desert, past sparse vegetation and bone-dry water courses. Idres and Faysal were not at all fazed by the absence of a road. In summer, temperatures here frequently hit 45 degrees Centigrade but on that day it was a pleasant 35°C.

The only other signs of animal life were skinny camels chewing thoughtfully on desert thistles, pinched-looking goats and sheep and a few foraging gazelles. Occasionally we'd pass a lone man carrying a bucket of water on his head and making his way to one of the small eruptions of local real estate which comprised head-high shacks covered in discarded UN food sacks.

We lurched and bumped along for an hour before we reached the Djibouti side of the border and stopped in a flurry of sand in the middle of a village of lean-tos and shacks that lined the road. Faysal swung into action and rounded up the immigration officers from under a thatched shelter which was the local café. Because it was Friday the border was closed and it took some skilled negotiation on Faysal's part and a chunk of baksheesh

($US150 for each side of the border) on ours to get them to attend to us. Meanwhile the villagers had gathered around. We took digital photographs and showed them the images. At first they were suspicious but when they recognised our goodwill they clamoured for a turn in front of the camera.

129 Somalia

We walked the 500 metres across no-man's-land to the Somalia side of the border and were met by a loose-limbed man in a grey T-shirt and sandals, whom we took to be the head Somali immigration officer.

Close to a concrete hut with a barred window, which doubled as the lock-up and the immigration office, a group of men were squatting under a large acacia tree. 'Sit over here with us,' the officer indicated with slow hand gestures. The men were chewing on qat leaves, a local stimulant, and offered us some. It tasted peppery and bitter.

The news of our photography had crossed the border before we did, and in moments all the people of the village, amid a lot of self-deprecating giggling, were begging to be on camera.

Though dressed in piecemeal clothing, the Somalis were fine-looking people – tall, sensual, dignified and endowed with good humour. Some of the women were particularly beautiful, their delicate features and glowing skins framed by elegantly swathed headscarves.

At one point the crowd parted and stood quietly to allow the village chairman to make his way over to us. Ahmed Omar Gouled was a man of presence. He wore a white jacket, cloth skullcap and a blue skirt. A folded blanket was draped over one shoulder and in the other hand he carried a gnarled walking stick.

He extended his hand. 'Welcome,' he said in good English and indicated we must sit opposite each other. Chairman Gouled was a handsome man even though deep lines cut through his features and I guessed him to be in his 60s. He sat straight-backed and dignified, smiling gently. He wished to have his photograph taken with his grandson, and would we be able to send photographs to the villagers when we returned home. We walked with him to a small hut to write down his address.

'This is the village shop,' he said proudly. 'I am the owner.' He indicated the spartan display of tins and packets. We thanked him for his welcome and made our way back to the border. A gaggle of villagers fell in behind me, making me feel like the Pied Piper.

On the return journey to Djibouti our guides tuned the radio to an Islamic religious station. We became hypnotised by the rhythmic chanting, the heat and the monotony of the desert. Our visit to Somalia had been a heart-warming experience.

Idres turned to me and asked, 'Do you mind if we pray?' We turned west and came to a ramshackle group of houses. Before us was a mosque which in the poor surroundings looked almost grand. Faysal washed his feet under a tap and went inside and for 30 minutes we waited by the truck returning the waves and smiles of worshippers as they came by.

Back in Djibouti we took a day room at the Sheraton to try to catch up on some sleep. But the mid-afternoon snore-off was disturbed by a pounding on the door by five hulky, grim-looking German Army personnel who were 'cleansing the floor' for the arrival that evening of the German Minister of Defence. This explained the presence at the airport of a grey camouflaged Luftwaffe A320. It did not reveal why a representative of a country that had decided not to participate in the build-up for war in Iraq was consorting with the Americans in one of the many strongholds of its armed forces.

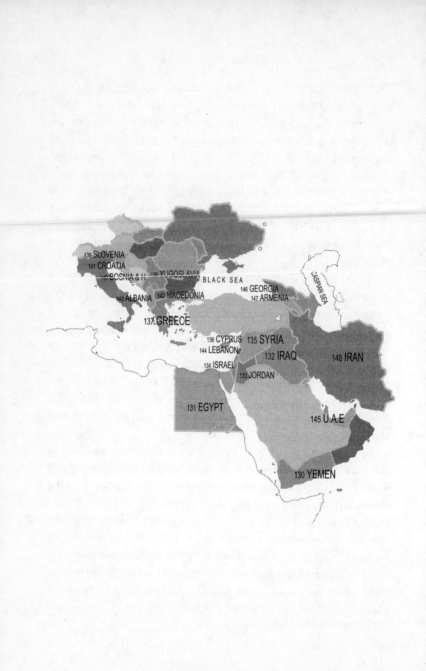

139 SLOVENIA
141 CROATIA
BOSNIA & H. 138 YUGOSLAVIA   BLACK SEA
143 ALBANIA   142 MACEDONIA   146 GEORGIA
                                           147 ARMENIA
137 GREECE
                136 CYPRUS   135 SYRIA
144 LEBANON   132 IRAQ   148 IRAN
134 ISRAEL
                133 JORDAN
131 EGYPT
                                       145 U.A.E
                              130 YEMEN

CASPIAN SEA

190

CHAPTER FIFTEEN

MIDDLE EAST

130 Yemen

At the airport a few hours later as we waited for the flight to Sana'a we talked to Paula and her colleague Tony. We didn't leave until the early hours of the morning and their keeping us company was a very hospitable gesture.

We waited on the Yemenia 737-800 for half an hour while a Hercules on the tarmac was being unloaded. Judging by the number of heavily-armed American soldiers surrounding it there must have been something seriously important coming off that plane.

We landed in Yemen at about 3.40 a.m. In the immigration queue I talked to a young woman in full black burkha. She spoke good English and told me she had been studying in the USA. She wasn't married.

'How would your future husband know what you look like if he can't see you?' I said, indicating her garb.

'He will have to judge me from what I say,' she said, and her dark eyes twinkled at me.

Security screening at the airport was protracted and thorough; armed soldiers were present at most intersections and major buildings on the drive to our hotel.

The walled city of Sana'a is one of the oldest cities in the world, and its mosques and public buildings are straight out of centuries past. Yemen's not considered a place in which to linger. In the past it was unsafe because of civil war between the north and the south. Now its volatility relates to protests against Israel. The Yemeni government is co-operative on the war against terrorism but many citizens express their anger with the US. The US, on the other hand, warned that a significant number of Al Qaeda operatives lived in Yemen and travel was extremely inadvisable: those already in the country should keep their heads down and leave as soon as they could.

We ran another gauntlet of security checks at the hotel. Our bags were rifled, our passports scrutinised, our persons patted. At any moment, I thought, they'd rummage through my hair.

'Does all this checking mean you have a lot of problems here?' I asked the night manager, a fussily efficient man in a suit that was too small for him.

'No, saab. They are precisely why we do not have a problem,' he said.

131 Egypt

Early in the morning we drove past the taupe-coloured, flat-roofed buildings of the town to a very quiet airport to take the flight to Cairo and, aboard an A310-300, were lifted into a clear insipid sky. The route took us over the top end of the vivid blue

Red Sea. On either side the desert glowed like an exaggerated painting. I was going to miss this thirsty, sprawling, infinitely fascinating part of the world.

Anna and Nic were in Cairo. They had arrived there a week before from New Zealand and I had 24 hours of family time with them before moving on. James spent the time pottering through the colourful, noisy, polluted, swarming streets of the city.

132 Iraq

The only airline flying into Iraq from that part of the world was Royal Jordanian which left from Amman and so, after assuring Anna and Nic I'd see them in Dubai for Christmas, James and I flew to Jordan.

We'd been keen to stay the night in Baghdad, but at Amman airport we found that our Iraqi visas (written in Arabic) had expired two days before. We'd have to go in and out on the same plane.

The flight was full: a group of Norwegian Red Cross workers carrying oversized parcels; businessmen from the Arab world; a handful of Iraqis; journalists and photographers, including a few Americans who were keeping very quiet. The first thing we saw as we disembarked in Baghdad was a large message in blood red letters roughly painted on the floor of the airbridge: 'Down with the USA.'

The airport was up-to-date with well-stocked duty-free stores, clean food outlets and, surprisingly, an abundance of alcohol. We repaired to a bar for a beer and at first were completely ignored. We talked loudly and mentioned New Zealand several times. A thin, stick-limbed barman with a bristling moustache slid over to us. 'You are from New Zealand?' he said, his eyebrows raised. 'I thought you were American. What can I get you?' And from then on we were treated to warm smiles and nods.

As we sipped our beer, passengers from two charter flights walked past. Our barman mate told us they were Iraqi pilgrims. They were shabbily dressed and carrying nothing. We wondered if they were pilgrims or returning refugees. Things being as they were in this part of the world you'd think they'd have flown anywhere but home.

We explained to Ammar Mohammed, an official from the Ministry of Protocol, that we were returning to Jordan on the same plane. He showed no surprise, obtained our boarding passes without a fuss and was happy to have his photograph taken beneath one of many large images of a young-looking Saddam Hussein that hung on the walls. With their dark hair, brooding good looks and heavy moustaches, the two men could have been brothers.

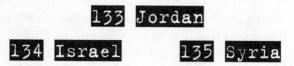

Back in Amman, just five hours after we had left it, we had time to look around.

Except in the old town, the city was crammed with apartments, houses, office buildings, hotels and a chaotic muddle of traffic. There was a lot of construction under way which apparently was to accommodate the 600,000 Jordanians who had returned from Kuwait after the last Gulf War. There's not a lot to recommend Amman but in this part of the world all roads seem to lead there and so it became our base to get into Syria and Israel.

The plan for the next day was to make a leisurely drive to the Israeli border, which we calculated was about 45 minutes' drive away. Then we would return and catch an evening flight to Damascus in Syria. We were far too ambitious. The route was across sizeable mountains, the weather cold, the road icy and a thick fog blanketed the landscape. Our driver was a 60-something, chubbily good-looking, chain-smoking Syrian called Imar.

'I have to take you a longer way,' he said, 'because the usual border is only for locals.'

We came to the fertile Jordan Valley. All in all, the journey we thought would take 45 minutes ended up taking two hours. We would not be flying to Damascus that night.

There was a bonus, however. As we had driven north we passed the lofty arch of Hadrian's Gate in the beautifully preserved Roman ruins of Jerash, about 50 kilometres north of Amman. Jerash was part of Emperor Pompey's league of commercial cities that he set up throughout the Middle East and was built around the third century AD. Only a small percentage of it has been excavated but already uncovered are monumental temples, churches, mosques, cathedrals, theatres, plazas and hippodromes.

When we finally reached the border at dusk it became apparent that, although a peace accord was signed between Jordan and Israel in 1994, no one was taking any chances. Imar could not drive us past the Jordanian border post and so we waited for a bus to take us the 500 metres to the Israeli side. Its driver, facing Mecca with his forehead pressed into his mat, was praying hard on the forecourt of the transfer station. And there he remained for the next 20 minutes.

Security was zealous. We signed reams of papers and then in the bus we drove past multiple rows of barbed wire and concrete barriers to a narrow gate which only one vehicle at a time could fit through. Two officers climbed aboard and demanded to know why we were coming to Israel. The underbelly of the bus was searched with spotlights and mirrors. We were ordered off the bus and our luggage was screened and rescreened then physically searched. All the electronic equipment was removed and then the bags were screened again. Only then were we allowed through to passport control where two young Israeli women in fatigues filled in the rest of the documentation.

By the time this was over all other travellers had gone and the bus would return to Jordan only when there were more than two people to make the trip worthwhile. We begged and eventually bribed the driver to take us back straight away.

On the way back to Amman we stopped for a small cup of thick black coffee at a kerbside café. It sustained us perfectly. Before the Gulf War the road and its surrounds had all been productive farmland. Now it was developed with housing and light industry. We passed one Palestine refugee camp after another. They were just like large suburbs. The Palestinians have been here so long that they have been permitted to build their own houses and set up businesses.

Upon our return I asked Imar to take us to the Syrian border the next day, a distance of about 120 kilometres. Much of eastern and northern Jordan is known as the East Bank, and is arid desert baked dry by temperatures that in summer are consistently in the 40s. This same waterless wilderness stretches into Iraq, Saudi Arabia and Syria, so as we headed north we passed through the city of Salt but little else. The primary feel of that land was of unbounded emptiness with hardly a goat or camel to be seen this side of the brown horizon.

Despite Western warnings about travelling to Syria we were sorry we were not going to be staying in Damascus which is said to be a collection of fascinating, time-worn and often elegant ruins of occupations past. Instead, we drove straight to the airport, past the run-down, dirty, more modern bits where the only colour was provided by massive amounts of signage on the sides of the road.

Our tickets onward to Cyprus had been cancelled by Syrian Airlines. This was for the third time in two days. There was, however, one seat left which James insisted I take, knowing that his wait on stand-by would probably be brief.

And so regretfully and as suspected we left the Middle East. It had been notable that throughout the region anti-American feeling had not been particularly overt, although people were definitely friendlier to us once they knew we were not from the States. But threats of an invasion of Iraq were having a devastating effect on the tourist trade. No one was travelling there. In Cairo there were only a few European tourists to be seen, in Yemen and Syria none at all. Visitor numbers in Jordan had dropped about 70 percent in the last year. It must have been really tough for the thousands of people whose modest incomes depended on tourist dollars.

And yet we had not felt a trace of hostility directed at us. We'd never felt threatened, and the people we met were remarkably generous, honest and friendly.

I vowed that sometime soon I'd return to the Middle East and get to know it better.

CHAPTER SIXTEEN

THE BALKANS
AND MIDDLE EAST

The airport at Greek-held Larnaca in Cyprus had been converted from a domestic to an international airport because, in 1974, the island's international airport was lost to Turkey along with 40 percent of the northeast end of this island.

We knew we'd left the Middle East when we heard Christmas carols playing over the intercom and the airport was hung with decorations, but we had little time to appreciate them before we were boarding Cyprus Airways A319-100 to fly on to Athens.

Athens airport is a substantial new edifice, connected to the city by a recently completed eight-lane, 35-kilometre highway.

Both have been built for the Olympics to be held here in 2004. But at 11 p.m. we didn't want to go anywhere particularly when we had to be back at the airport at 6.45 next morning. We stayed at the Sofitel Hotel at the airport, which was also brand-new.

138 Yugoslavia

To get to what is now known as the Union of Serbia and Montenegro, we crammed into a full Turkish Airlines RJ-70 Avroliner and flew a triangular route via Istanbul to disembark in Pristina, Kosovo, in a biting three degrees Centigrade with horizontal sleet coming at us like needles.

Funded by the United Nations, the terminal was being rebuilt. Even the half-finished part was freezing cold but it hummed with people. I sat on the floor, which was the only available space. Next to me stood a sleekly uniformed Sikh, his handsome head swathed in a pale blue turban. By way of introduction I said, 'Excuse me, sir, is that turban of yours bulletproof?'

He laughed and smoothed his coal-black beard with the palm of his hand. 'HP Singh,' he said, holding the same hand towards me. 'Indian police force. I am here on a two-year assignment with the UN Mission in Kosovo.'

HP lived at the UN airforce base at Camp Bondsteel, one of 4,000 UN personnel in the Kosovo region.

'The UN is in complete administrative control at the moment,' he said, 'and it will remain here until 2006 to train local people to take over. When the Serbs left there was nobody trained to do the job.'

He was feeling the cold in Kosovo. So was I, and our departure to Slovenia on an Adria Airways Airbus 320, an hour after we had landed, was delayed because the wings had to be de-iced before it could leave the ground. As we rose into the metal-grey sky, any view we might have had of Kosovo through the window of the plane was blurred by a mosaic of frozen crystals.

139 Slovenia

Ljubljana is a wonderful city. At this time of the year snow covered the ground, Christmas decorations filled the shops, colourful Christmas trees were on every corner and the city's fountains were wrapped like presents. Through the city runs the languid Ljubljana River with baroque buildings lining its embankments. It's often referred to as White City because of its pale-coloured churches and mansions, built during the time of the Habsburgs.

We made our way to the Grand Hotel. The rate was more than we had been told. I drew myself up and glared down at the very short Turkish desk clerk. 'That's too much,' I said. 'If you can't do better I'll have to go next door to the Holiday Inn.'

Completely unruffled, he glared back at me from under thick black eyebrows, smiled disarmingly and said, 'As you wish, sir, but you'll be back. It is much more expensive. I know this because we own both hotels.'

We woke next morning to a clear bright sky. Before we flew on to Bosnia-Hercegovina we climbed a 90-metre hill up to a fairytale castle that guards the maze of narrow streets making up the old town. The city below us looked like a miniature Prague or Salzburg surrounded by manicured countryside, lakes and mountains.

Slovenia had the good sense to break away from Yugoslavia in 1991 and has since enjoyed peace and relative prosperity. It is a stunningly beautiful country, affluent, uncrowded, rich in resources and on the sunny side of the Alps.

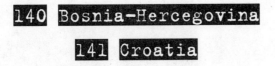 140 Bosnia-Hercegovina
141 Croatia

The newly-built Butmic Airport outside Sarajevo in Bosnia-Hercegovina was a palace compared to the airport at Pristina. Like the rest of the city it had been reconstructed by United Nation's funding, whose presence was still very much in evidence. Getting a visa for this country had been a difficult and drawn-out effort, and then when we got to immigration, the officer just waved us through without even bothering to look at it.

Within an hour we were flying on to Zagreb in Croatia. It was dusk as we drove into the city for the night, and in the gathering gloom I conjured up the terrible spectre of the mayhem and massacres that had not so long ago sullied the roadsides in this part of the world. We left again at dawn and what little we saw of the city seemed plain and weary after the fresh beauty of Ljubljana.

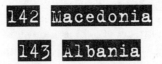 142 Macedonia
143 Albania

I can't describe the Skopje airport because the whole time we were there we were surrounded by a jostling, braying mob of taxi drivers who formed a bobbing sea of black leather jackets beneath clouds of cigarette smoke.

Here we met Sammi or, more to the point, Sammi found us. He was a muscled, swarthily handsome young man sporting a three-day stubble, and spoke a smattering of English. Such were his charms that we hired him to take us to the Kontinental hotel that night and next day to drive us west to the Albanian border and then on to Greece.

Macedonian border with Albania.

The day dawned clear and very cold. We scraped up some nourishment in the restaurant, where we were outnumbered by chain-smoking waiters, and met Sammi outside the hotel. I struck a bargain with him: if he drove carefully and we made it to the Greek border, not only alive but satisfied that he'd driven safely, he would earn a substantial bonus. And so the first part of the journey was peppered with his anxious enquiries. 'I drive okay?'

Then about 30 km out of Skopje, going up a hill, he suddenly slammed on the brakes. James yelled, I hit the front seat and a rock as big as a football came bouncing down the steep slope and smashed into the front of the car.

Sammi, his broad shoulders flicking with irritation, walked back down the road to pick up his front bumper, light surrounds, grill and number plate. He was not so obliging when he came back. 'Bonus not good,' he yelled. 'I go faster, I not here. Now I spend six bonuses to mend.' He attempted to reaffix some of the items to the front of his VW Passat and then drove off with most of them in the boot.

Sammi's mood did not improve when only a few kilometres on he was pulled over by a traffic officer for not displaying his

The rock had gone, but the damage remained, Macedonia.

number plate. We sat submissively in the car and watched him talking hard, waving his hands about like protesting doves. He was enacting a blow-by-blow description of events, which no doubt included a lament that he'd ever met a certain pair of New Zealanders. He took the officer by the arm and opened the boot to show him the evidence. The two men jiggled with laughter and the officer waved us on. Humour restored to pre-rock-disaster level, we continued in peace through a snow-spangled, ruggedly beautiful countryside. By the side of the road clusters of skiers were waiting for mountain buses.

A hundred kilometres later we pulled up at the stone-grey wall that indicated the border crossing at Povadec, where we were stamped out of Macedonia by a young, friendly woman who indicated that we must walk to Albania on foot.

We strode off in temperatures that were well below zero into a wind that bit into my skin like tigers' teeth. That insane five-minute ski-walk on ice through no-man's-land felt like twenty. But insanity seemed agreeable enough to the police at the Albanian post. A young woman, neat and businesslike in her navy uniform, beckoned us to follow her to a small room to be stamped out of the country. Her name was Alma Hahsallayari. The room was agreeably warm and we made the most of it while we were issued with visas and stamps, which is probably why we lived to return to Macedonia.

I was taking photographs as we approached the Macedonian border again and received a lecture from an irate border policeman. As he was bawling me out a diminuitive, pale-faced Albanian man waiting in the queue stepped forward. 'Let me help you,' he said. 'My name is Kledi Milloshi. I am the senior translator at Camp Bondsteel in Kosovo.' He turned to the officer and rattled off some long explanation with evident success. Kledi accepted our offer to come with us to the Greek border and then return to Skopje with Sammi when we went on to Thessaloniki.

We turned south and arrived at the town of Ohrid, Macedonia's delightful tourist Mecca built on the edge of the lake of the same name. Lake Ohrid is the deepest lake in Europe, a large rocky bowl of crystal-clear water surrounded by high mountains. The town's many monuments and churches, the tiled roofs of its Italianate villas on the folded hills and the backdrop of jagged peaks made it look like a cross between Como and Queenstown.

Despite the crisp air we sat at a streetside table outside a small café. A small child of about six, his head cosied in a brightly-coloured beanie, slid around the tables with his palm out. Kledi translated his story. His parents had died when he was one. His grandma looked after him and he needed money for her medicine. I snapped him for the children's book and he told me via Kledi that his dream was that his grandmother would be able to make decisions for him forever. He earned himself $US5 for her medicine.

We drove on through Bitola, a bleak, damp city and the coldest in Macedonia, then through a number of long brick tunnels decorated with thick stalactites, and half an hour later arrived at the Greek border at Gevgelija. Sammi had earned his bonus. He beamed his thanks and we wished him and Kledi a safe rock-free journey home.

James and I, wearing every bit of clothing we possessed, began to trudge through a kilometre of grit and slush. Hunched against the bone-chilling cold, we shivered and slid our way into Greece.

144 Lebanon

In a small taverna attached to the immigration post, clutching mugs of coffee, we gradually thawed out while we waited for a taxi to take us to Thessaloniki airport about 120 kilometres away. We cruised the distance at an unnerving 140 km/h which delivered us four hours ahead of departure; and then we almost missed the flight through Athens to Beirut because we'd failed to observe the time change.

It was 3 a.m. when we arrived at Beirut's contemporary airport. We would only be there for four hours but we needed a hotel and a sleep. We shuffled out to the taxi rank and were ushered towards the oldest Mercedes in the rank and the oldest driver, a hunched little man with an enormous drooping moustache. 'Sheraton hotel,' I said.

'No Sheraton,' said Moustache.

'Yes,' I said.

'No, no Sheraton.'

'The Sheraton,' I said, in my 'I'm-in-charge voice'.

He shrugged and 10 minutes later we pulled up outside the Lancaster hotel. 'No Sheraton,' said Moustache, grinning. 'Lancaster was Sheraton.'

Five hours later on the way back to the airport I took a few photographs of Beirut, once the Paris of the Middle East and now recovering from 17 years of war. There were signs of destruction alongside rebuilding and attractive old architecture; space as well as overcrowding; spanking-new cars and handcarts; old alleys alongside new highways.

Leaden with exhaustion, I could hardly lift the camera. James and I were both unclean and unshaven and thus we flew towards the United Arab Emirates, Christmas, and the arms of our families, feeling as if we'd crossed the world on foot.

145 United Arab Emirates

For Christmas in Dubai we were joining our friends Peter and Geli and their two children Oliver and Alissa for three days. Nicola, Anna and Nic arrived from the Southern Hemisphere and Egypt respectively.

Dubai has some of the most over-the-top architecture in the world with buildings becoming more and more grand and opulent in a bid to outdo each other. Peter, a New Zealander, is the general manager of the Grand Hyatt. This staggeringly large hotel was still under construction but a good example of the local style. Like a miniature city the new hotel had 600 rooms, hundreds of apartments and 14 restaurants, a huge ballroom, gold inlay in all ceilings and walls, a spa the size of a large house, squash courts, several swimming pools, separate kitchens for pork, fish and meat dishes, an ice carving room . . . on and on.

We stayed at the original and more humble Hyatt Apartments, and in the adjacent carpark next afternoon we joined about 4,000 other spectators, all Pakistanis, to watch a Kashmiri wrestling match.

On Christmas day we went four-wheel-drive 'dune bashing' over the huge rusty-red sand mountains of the desert to the south of Dubai. The weather was surprisingly chilly and the sand damp from scattered falls of rain. Christmas dinner was in a faux Bedouin desert camp, which was really just a patch of sand surrounded by brush fence with a bar to one side and shelter under brightly patterned awnings. We lazed around on thick Persian rugs and colourful cushions, ate barbecued lamb kebabs, chicken, tabbouleh and hummus, and toasted our good fortune.

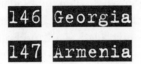

146 Georgia
147 Armenia

Christmas over, we flew with Anna and Nicola still in tow (Nic had returned to New Zealand) to Tbilisi and an airport covered in snow and ice. Outside the terminal we whistled up a taxi – a Lada of incalculable years – but we had to wait while the elderly, corpulent, out-of-breath driver tottered off with a plastic bottle to buy petrol, leaving us huddled and freezing in the car's tatty interior. He came back with a full bottle which he emptied into the petrol tank and we set forth on the 20-minute ride to Tbilisi. Whenever we topped a rise, the driver muttered his thanks to the engine, slipped the gear into neutral and we coasted down the other side. The classic petrol-saving manoeuvre.

Because flights in and out of Georgia were infrequent, we had to stay at Tbilisi for nearly three days in temperatures that hovered around minus 11 degrees Centigrade. Our base was the Sheraton in the rebuilt old part of town. Everthing was in darkness when we arrived. The desk clerk apologised: 'We are saving electricity,' he said. He then turned on so many lights we felt embarrassed that we were plundering the national grid.

The presence of the US Army was not evident in Tbilisi. At breakfast next morning I began talking to an elderly American who said he was a civilian contractor to the US Army. 'We are training the Georgian Army,' he said. 'The government's defence budget is $28 million, which is such a small amount that the United States is helping out.' The main reason, we suspect, is to ensure that the oil pipeline being built from Azerbaijan to

Turkey through Georgia goes unmolested.

In the warm hospitable air of civilised Dubai, Anna and Nicola had been enthusiastic about joining us, but here in Georgia with all its deprivations they were having second thoughts. It was no surprise when they told us they would not be joining us next day for the road journey to Armenia.

Our vehicle was upgraded to a Land Rover, thankfully, for much of the road south was furrowed, potholed, scattered with rocks and surfaced with thick black ice. But my abiding image is of the tough little Ladas and Volgas we passed on the way. They were dented and filthy with cracked windscreens, roofs laden with bundles and luggage stuffed so tightly into their boots that the lids had to be tied down with string. And every one of them was crammed with peering, chain-smoking, bulky Georgian men. Thus burdened, these stoic little cars battled along the appalling road, at a cracking speed, splattering the donkeys hauling cartfuls of faggots.

Intermittently rows of Russian-designed, multi-storeyed, apartment blocks appeared. They had the architectural flair of a brick and were as desolate as the land they perched on. The only colour came from washing hanging hopefully from the balconies. Electricity supply was at best infrequent so most apartments had installed wood-burning stoves and punched jerry-rigged flumes through windows to the outside. Balconies were stacked with firewood.

On open land, dry stalks poked through the snow and fat-tailed sheep foraged around thorn bushes, but we also passed large areas of wintering grapes which brought our joke-loving London ambassador to mind. Close to the Armenian border the road degenerated further into a muddy sludge. A heavy truck was bogged to its axles.

We explained our mission to the Georgian border guard by showing him the Russian version of Phil Goff's letter and then we slipped and slithered across no-man's-land into Armenia, where we persuaded Artur to take us to his warm and comfortable hut to stamp our passports. He offered us a cup of strong sweet coffee and mineral water, and we spoke of Armenia's war with Azerbaijan.

'I thought things had settled down,' I said.

He wiggled his hand as if to say, 'Maybe.'

On the way back to Tbilisi again we stopped in some of the shabby villages along the way. Shops had been set up in rusting caravans or old truck cabs or under shelters of sacking and roofing iron battened down with boulders. Older people, swathed in jerseys, scarves and rugs, squatted on bits of wood, warming themselves in front of coal-fire buckets and selling cigarettes and soap or heating their pots of evil-looking stew. We were told that rat's meat is often added to increase bulk.

At one place, a young boy wheeled a trussed sheep in a wheel-barrow to a large slab of concrete which served as an abattoir. A hefty man in a black beanie, his father presumably, slit the animal's throat and bled it into the dust. A mangy-looking dog sidled along and feasted on the blood. The carcase was hung and skinned and there it would remain until sold: there was no need for refrigeration in those temperatures. Even in Tbilisi meat was openly displayed in the street.

Foreigners are rare in Georgia in the freezing winter; and yet we experienced such warmth from the people that we'd both like to go back someday when the weather is more inviting.

When we left the country on 30 December, the inside of the airport terminal was actually colder than the carpark outside. Wearing every article of clothing in our possession we waited for our airliner looking, in Georgian fashion, like escaped Yetis.

Onboard the 30-year-old Russian YAK-40 bound for Azerbaijan, the crew were also Yeti-dressed and had to sit at the rear of the plane to give us aisle-room to get to our seats.

We overnighted in Baku again. On the way from the airport a man we'd met called Afgan Asgarov gave Anna a lift to the caviare black market. She returned to the hotel triumphantly bearing a pottle of Beluga caviare, which was a steal at $US20. We hadn't seen it in any of the four caviare-producing states around the Caspian Sea – Russia, Azerbaijan, Kazakhstan and Turkmenistan. The United Nations had given caviare exporters a quota ultimatum aimed at protecting the 'black gold' fish eggs, but I didn't like their chances. Since the disintegration of the Soviet Union, the once highly-regulated caviare industry had been overtaken by a lucrative black market: 250 grams of Caspian caviare will set you back about £1000 in London.

The next day I was able to show Anna something of the city that I had so fallen in love with before we caught an Azerbaijan Airlines 727-200 to Iran. The plane had been crudely hand-painted and there were brushmarks over surfaces. The serial number plate at the cabin entrance was so thickly painted that it couldn't be read. It made me think that the plane had been stolen.

148 Iran

At Tehran Airport as we waited to be let into the country we were approached by a lithe-looking man in a brown suit who politely introduced himself as the immigration manager. His face wore an expression of both warmth and the steely look of authority. 'It is important for your wives to cover their heads in this country,' he said as he relieved us of our passports, tickets and baggage tags.

I asked him how long he would be. 'When it is done,' he said, and escorted us upstairs to the departure lounge which was devoid of life except for a few airport workers asleep on the padded bench seats.

We dozed until midnight rolled around. Then alone in the huge hall we wished each other Happy New Year. From one of the duty-free stores a thickset man with broad shoulders and a beetling black moustache offered us a tray of Iranian sweets. 'It is not our custom, but Happy New Year,' he said, and disappeared again.

We felt rather small and alone. It was an odd place to spend New Year's Eve.

Later we were joined by two pompous Englishmen, Tom and Pete, who were from the United Kingdom Immigration Overseas Escorting Service and had just returned an overstayer to Iran. They had to wait it out at the airport because they had no visas.

'New Zealand is 30 years behind the rest of the world,' announced Tom.

'Have you been there?'

'Well no, but so they say.'

When later the Emirates crew said that the British Airways flight had been delayed for 24 hours, I was secretly rather pleased. I ordered myself a whisky to celebrate Tom's 24 hours in a country not 30 years behind, but centuries.

176 JAPAN
175 N. KOREA
174 S. KOREA
173 MONGOLIA
172 CHINA
171 TAIWAN
170 PHILIPPINES
177 PALAU
169 BRUNEI
160 MALAYSIA
158 SINGAPORE
159 INDONESIA
157 VIETNAM
156 CAMBODIA
155 LAOS
154 THAILAND
153 MYANMAR
151 BHUTAN
152 BANGLADESH
150 NEPAL
149 INDIA
168 SRI LANKA
167 MALDIVES
161 PAKISTAN
162 OMAN
163 KUWAIT
164 BAHRAIN
166 QATAR
165 SAUDI ARABIA
CASPIAN SEA
BLACK SEA

CHAPTER SEVENTEEN

ASIA

149 India

We finally left Tehran at 4.30 a.m. of the first day of 2003, and set down in Dubai airport two hours later to await an onward flight to Delhi. There are worse places to be marooned for a few hours than in the-over-the-top Dubai airport with its cavernous opulence, potted palm trees and luxurious carpet patterned with sand dunes. But because I hadn't slept and Anna and Nicola were leaving, I decided to take myself back to the Hyatt apartments and snatch four hours' sleep. James opted to stay at the airport to see Nicola off. At 1 p.m., feeling only marginally refreshed, I returned to the airport to find him sitting in the departure lounge like a mummified fish. Because of fog in Jaipur, where the plane was coming from, our flight did not leave until 6 p.m. that night. It crossed my mind that the wait might have been a karmic lesson from Pommy Tom. I'd still rather wait in Dubai.

Indian Airlines does not offer the newest or cleanest plane, nor a crew chosen for their youthful looks, but they make up for it by placing within easy reach copious miniature bottles of whisky.

In Delhi we were met by Jadesh, the tall, clean-cut airport representative for the Hyatt Regency. I knew him well, as this was about my 12th visit to Delhi. It had been a favourite haunt of mine when Peter had been general manager of the hotel before he went to Dubai.

'Ha, Mr John, you are back,' he said, grinning delightedly. I learned later that it was his day off and once again felt guilty for his kindness.

The reason we were in Delhi was to link with a flight to Bhutan. This had not been easy. Druk Air does not belong to IATA (International Air Transport Association) and it had taken around 50 emails to book a flight direct. Now we had to pay for the tickets. Jadesh led us all over the airport looking for the Druk Air office which we eventually stumbled across at the end of an unmarked corridor only to find it was securely padlocked. There was nothing for it but to head for the hotel to make the most of a mere four-hour break. But we had a reprieve. The airport was fogged in and our flight would not be leaving for at least five hours.

One hour had passed when James' phone whined. It was the Druk airport manager, Raju Chitraker. 'You must be here within 45 minutes,' he said. I peered out the hotel window. There was still zero visibility. Drowsy and dishevelled, we fumbled our way to a taxi and the driver found the airport by using either a Braille map or a remarkable memory.

Without tickets we were not allowed to enter the terminal; the tickets were inside at the Druk office. James persuaded the guard to let him go alone to get them while I waited outside. Once we'd been admitted, we found Raju Chitrakar. 'There is no way this fog is going to lift,' I said. 'I bet you fifty dollars we won't be going today.'

'Too much,' he said. 'I'll bet you a drink of your choice.'

Three hours later the fog lifted slightly. Raju ventured onto the tarmac, waving his arms around as though searching blindly for the plane. He came back and begged us to make haste.

'I'm not going out there to sit on a plane that's not going anywhere,' I said.

Raju looked horrified. 'You must come. Yes, yes, Mr John, it is going now.'

It did; and thanks to Raju's insistence we were on it. He never did get to choose his drink.

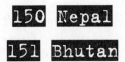

150 Nepal

151 Bhutan

We flew into Kathmandu but saw nothing of the ramparts and terraced hillsides that surround the city. It was just a featureless spread of buildings wrapped in a heavy polluted gauze – a bit like Old Delhi on drugs. We were not sorry to just touch the ground and fly on.

We sent a note to the cockpit and Captain Choeda came to meet us and witness our presence in Kathmandu. He was a handsome caramel-skinned man with a warm face and slanting eyes, typical of the Indian-Mongolian look of the Drukpas of Bhutan.

The weather had cleared and we took to the air to fly east, parallel to the Himalayas. The endless ranges of gargantuan peaks looked freshly laundered by the first snows of winter that had fallen during the night. The sky was crystalline blue.

As the pinnacle of Mt Everest came into view, the purser brought me a message from Captain Choeda. Would I like to sit up front for the landing? Would I ever.

And so, strapped to the jump seat, I had one of the most amazing experiences of my life.

I looked to the front and was horrified to see that we were

heading straight for a mountain. Then the nose of the plane tipped up and we skimmed over the top with a warning signal screaming: 'Terrain, terrain.' I looked at the altimeter. It read 16,000 feet.

'Disregard, disregard,' intoned the pilot, calmly. To our left a towering buttress of shaggy rock soared skyward: perched on a ledge 900 metres up from the valley floor was Tiger's Nest (Takishang) monastery, the most spectacular monastery in Bhutan, marking the site where Guru Rinpoche landed when he flew into Tibet on the back of a tiger and brought Buddhism to Bhutan.

We headed straight for another mountain, banked right, descended and skimmed down a steeply-sided V-shaped valley; banked right and zoomed along another, the starboard wing a mere 15 metres from the flanks of the mountain and ahead, perched on a knoll, was a house with a chimney which was the marker for the Paro airport beyond. We swept over it at 50 feet and landed with barely a bump on the runway, which is considered to be the most challenging commercial landing pad in the world.

Cheoda cupped his hands and offered up a prayer. 'Today was easy,' he said. 'Keeping control of the plane in the shearing winds that often whip through can be difficult.'

We'd been a little contemptuous about the Druk Airlines BAE-146 aircraft. BAE was said to be an acronym for 'bring another engine'. But for peak performance in this startling part of the world, its four-engine, high-wing design was perfect.

We had 24 hours in Bhutan and it was evident that the difficulties we'd had getting visas and flight reservations were due to offhand representation in Australasia, not to the Drukpas' reluctance to welcome us to their Buddhist country.

This formerly aloof nation opened its gates to visitors in 1974. At first allowing only 1000 a year, it now aimed for 15,000 low-impact, high-revenue tourists. Visitors were accompanied by a representative from Bhutan Tourism who controlled everything from transport and accommodation to what they saw and where they ate. This ensured, we were told, that during the recommended one-week stay (two if infirm) they saw as much as possible. Unfortunately we were there for only one day.

The tiny kingdom of Bhutan, squeezed between China and India, was only about the size of Denmark. Its incumbent ruler was King Jigme Singye Wangchuck, whose policy of controlled development ensured that new buildings were built in the traditional style and that preservation of the environment and the unique culture is paramount. Focus was also on economic self-reliance and what the king called 'Gross National Happiness'. Profit was not as important as things such as providing everyone with free education and free medical care. There was no unemployment and everybody had a house with a reasonable plot of land.

Happiness was evident in the serene, smiling eyes of the Drukpas. They mostly wore the traditional knee-length wraps which have a tartan-like pattern with large white cuffs.

Typical of the Drukpas' gentle disposition was our guide Prem Ghanley, who took us on a tour of Paro's hinterland, one of the most beautiful towns we'd ever seen. Everywhere, protected in ornate structures, there were prayer-wheels, some of which were so large that they held thousands of prayers. 'The wheel must be spun clockwise,' said Prem, 'so that prayers can be thrown forward into the wind.'

Then, pointing to the precipitous slopes of the mountain covered in pine trees, he said: 'Up in the mountains there are many yaks. They provide milk, cheese and meat, and their hair is used to make rope. But they can only live above 3000 feet.' We were yakless down in the town but saw plenty of the squat, shaggy little ponies which are a common form of transport.

A group of aspiring bowmen were practising the national sport of archery on a patch of stony ground near the river. As soon as they had fired an arrow they walked forward to retrieve it from the target. How no one was pierced from behind was a mystery.

That night we were bidden to stay at Olathang Hotel, which was the best hotel in Paro, despite being a rather rural three-star. The all-up price of $US200 per person per day to stay in the country included everything except alcohol. In the hotel dining room that night we ate a hearty meal of rice, chicken, roast pork and green beans.

The next day dawned stunningly clear. Mist rose gently off the mountains and a soft zephyr puffed its way through the town. In that kind of weather, Paro was probably the most peaceful place on earth.

At the airport waiting for our flight out we shared the lounge with the sister of the Queen of Bhutan. She was a short, plump woman surrounded by an entourage of her countrymen who, with great respect, kept her at a distance from us mere mortals.

Kolkata (Calcutta) was as chaotic as always. The social horrors of the city have not diminished – the awful poverty, fetid water courses, trash, wandering cows, disintegrating buildings, ornate shrines, slums and a continual ear-bashing din. Through this hurly-burly tiny Suzukis and majestic Ambassadors wove through the dense traffic and rickshaws pulled by skinny, sweating coolies gasping in the polluted atmosphere.

It sounds appalling and in part it is; and yet there is also charm in its vitality and glaring contrasts. Among the mayhem appears humour and art and smiling generosity; new buildings and palm trees and verdant parklands such as Eden Gardens and the famous Calcutta Cricket Ground.

We didn't know where we were staying so we wrote Sheraton on the immigration form. 'Would that be Sheraton Mumbai?' asked the officer.

'That'd be a bloody long taxi ride from here,' I said, 'No, we're in the Sheraton Kolkata.'

He shrugged and ticked the form.

'The Sheraton, please,' I said to the taxi driver who snared us as we emerged from the terminal. He nodded and nosed his Ambassador into the traffic with ample use of the horn. After a kilometre James asked if he knew where the Sheraton was. 'No, sir. There's no Sheraton, sir. I am taking you to Hyatt Regency.'

'Oh.'

The hotel wasn't quite finished but it was the soft opening and for $US70 a night we had two opulent rooms in a palace which was in complete contrast to the overwhelming squalor of the city around us. But that's Kolkata.

152 Bangladesh

Kolkata airport's security screening was inept. After two hours of queuing and five screenings and pat-downs, a sixth guard, looking like a wood chopper, stepped towards me with a hand-held scanner. 'No,' I spat, 'I've had enough of this,' and walked toward the plane.

'Okay,' he chirped, 'have a good flight.'

We knew we could get visas for Bangladesh on arrival. Engulfed by an unco-ordinated mass of people we were told to wait 'over there', which we did – waited and waited. No joy there, so I went downstairs to the immigration desk, and was told to 'wait in that queue over there', which I did.

Thirty minutes later we headed the queue, behind a couple from the Netherlands who were having no luck trying to get a visa. We had, we felt, the same serious predicament.

'You should have got a visa from the embassy in your country,' said the corpulent little immigration chap wearily.

'Where in New Zealand is that?' I asked, stabbing at my passport.

He looked at the document studiously and then exclaimed,

'Oh my goodness, I am very sorry, sir. You are not from the Netherlands. You are from New Zealand. Please would you be so kind as to come through and fill out these forms.'

It still took an hour to get to the airport forecourt where we were greeted by the disconcerting sight of thousands of clamouring Bangladeshis pushing against a 2.5-metre iron-barred fence six metres away. But the first person to approach us wasn't a pleading taxi driver but the airport representative for the Sheraton. We'd again nominated that hotel without ascertaining its existence. We climbed into the van and lurched off through the streets of Dhaka which, like Kolkata's, were mayhem.

Dhaka, sited on the northern bank of the Buringanga River in the centre of Bangladesh, appalled the senses with its heat and decay, its penetrating odours, swarms of humanity, unholy din and sticky polluted air. Swallowed by the heaving confusion, we made our way towards a comfortable night's rest – this time in a Sheraton hotel.

James looked out his window and observed an impressive bit of recycling. Large bins of scraps had been left open to the skies, from where a throng of birds rapidly descended and demolished the ghastly feast in minutes.

On the way to the airport next day we had to change course to avoid an impossibly tangled rickshaw jam and saw first-hand why Dhaka is dubbed the rickshaw capital of the world. Around 300,000 of them jiggle through its streets every day.

The nation that had taken two hours for us to enter took 10 minutes to exit. Clearly, getting rid of people from this seriously overpopulated country is a priority. The hundreds of pilgrims leaving for Mecca were outnumbered by an army of manual labourers who, lured by the possibility of work, were leaving for various destinations in the Middle East.

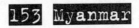 153 Myanmar

Biman Airlines had fitted out a new Airbus 310-300 with recycled and faulty seats and seat belts, but the Bangladeshi crew were charming. We saw a lot of rainforest and rugged wilderness as we flew across Myanmar towards Yangon (formerly Rangoon), and when we'd landed the crew allowed us to leave the plane to take a photograph even though cameras were forbidden. On the outside, the temple-shaped roofline of the terminal building was ornately carved and heavily festooned with faux-gold.

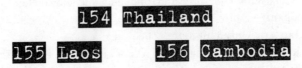 154 Thailand
155 Laos   156 Cambodia

A short time later we flew on to Bangkok which, after the airports we'd been to lately, was so organised and clean that it was a culture shock. I'd always enjoyed efficiency but now it just seemed boring. I took one look at the milling hordes of pale-skinned tourists, scanned the departure board for a way out and reserved seats on the next flight to Laos. We'd possibly set a record by entering and exiting the country in 10 minutes.

We landed near a bend of the Mekong River in Vientiane (pronounced Weng Chan) and were driven straight to the Lao Plaza Hotel, one of several good hotels in the town. At a super-ficial glance the city, with its plethora of little restaurants, street stalls, beer halls, night markets, handsome temples and streets seething with mopeds and pedestrians, looks like a Singapore or Kuala Lumpur of 30 years ago. We liked the feel of the place which still had a sense of the exotic, now missing from those larger cities.

Back at the airport in the morning we boarded a plane for Bangkok again, where we endured a five-hour stop-over. James had a haircut, an experience which demonstrated that the lascivious side of the city was as robust as ever. It started off innocently enough with a short back and sides. And then the cutter, a woman advancing without grace into her late 30s, pouted her cherry-red lips and rapped him on the genitals. 'And how about this,' she lisped.

'What?' said James, reeling from the shock.

'Very good. I give you very good.' She bared her teeth and tapped again.

'Thanks for the offer but I have no money,' said James.

'Very cheap, only 400 baht,' she said. Tap tap.

James pulled out his wallet, opened it and showed her its only occupant – a solitary $US10 note.

Tap tap. 'Only a bit more,' she said.

James glanced at his watch. 'Oh no, my plane. It's leaving.'

She shrugged. 'Okay. Good flight.'

We did – on to Phnom Penh, arriving as night overtook the city. Outside the terminal we met Mr Sam, taxi driver 20081, who politely greeted us, bowing from the waist: 'I'm very nice to meet you,' he said.

The next morning there was time to spare so I asked Mr Sam to drive us along beside the Mekong River. We cruised one highway which had been built by the Russians, another constructed by the United States and passed huge textile factories owned by the Chinese.

'Did the Cambodians build anything themselves?' I asked Mr Sam.

'Yes. They did. But not very good,' he said.

We rumbled down a dusty unsealed road past green fields splashed with colour from purple jacaranda trees and flowering bougainvillea.

We came to a stop outside the Choeung Ek Genocidal Centre, one of the many killing fields which the Khmer Rouge created on the outskirts of Phnom Penh. It featured an open-sided mausoleum where, on large trays of about 16 square metres, were piled the awful sight of dull-white human skulls. They were clinically categorised into infant, juvenile, adolescent, male and female piles, too sterile now for us to fully comprehend the scale of the horrors that put them there. Beside a series of mass graves were descriptions of how the bodies inside them had been found – without heads, or limbs or clothes. It seemed that children and females had been particularly mutilated.

One European couple was having trouble looking at all this. The woman tearfully forced herself to walk past the graves and then, ashen-faced, hurried away. A group of Cambodians was more accepting. They took it in turns to stand in front of the piles of skulls having their photographs taken.

Behind a fence of security wire a little ragged girl of about nine poked her hand past the barbs and with soulful eyes begged me for money. I took her photograph and gave her $US1. Her name was Ean but she didn't know her family name. Her dream was to work in the textile factory like all the other women.

Mr Sam drove us to the airport. It was built by the French.

157 Vietnam

Ho Chi Minh City was sprawling and polluted and, from the air, seemed to be without redeeming features. The roofs of the crowded buildings looked like rotting teeth. By now I'd seen enough of this part of the world to imagine the streams of bicycles, the bustle, the wealth and poverty, and the over-whelming bedlam that is Southeast Asia. We had a three-hour transit stop before flying on to Singapore.

158 Singapore

We'd been corresponding by Internet with a Kiwi couple, Kim and Todd Forrester, who had invited us to stay with them when we got to Singapore. They could have been axe murderers for all we knew, but we decided to take that chance.

Todd, a raw-boned man in a black T-shirt, was at Changi airport to welcome us and we took a taxi to the apartment in the Costa Rhu district that he shared with Kim and their son. 'You haven't eaten,' said Todd.

'Yes, we have,' I said.

'No, you haven't,' he said. 'I know it's 10 at night but Kim has been preparing food for most of the day.'

'Oh, right,' we chorused. 'We're famished.'

The meal was amazing – roast lamb and mint sauce, roast pumpkin, kumara, potatoes and fresh beans accompanied by two bottles of Villa Maria cabernet, with a highly decorated pavlova to follow. Half the apartment block of expats came to join us and we sat in the hot Singapore evening yarning as if we'd known each other all our lives. It felt as though we'd come home.

The only problem was that we'd only left ourselves three hours to sleep, and when the alarm went off at 6.30 a.m. I didn't hear it. I was woken half an hour later by James pounding in panic on my door.

My exit from Singpore, therefore, began at a charge and completely devoid of dignity.

159 Indonesia

The Silkair A320 was bound for Medan on the island of Sumatra in Indonesia. The city is unlikely to win an award for its aesthetic beauty, but I recommend it for the happy disposition of its people. It is the third largest in Indonesia, and a bit like Bangkok without tall buildings. There are some substantial old colonial-style homes from the Dutch days and many satellite dishes, motorcycles and rickshaws.

I hadn't showered for so long that I was beginning to offend myself, so James and I left the airport with a taxi driver called Uywda and in the humid heat rattled off to a hotel willing to accommodate my overdue need for cleaning.

After some hard negotiation over the rate I booked into the three-star Dirga Surya hotel and, ensconced in a large beige-on-beige bedroom with a faded picture of the Grand Canal of Venice on the wall, derobed for a cold shower (there was no hot water). Then primped to something near perfection, we raced back to the airport in time to catch our flight to Malaysia.

As it turned out, in plenty of time. The Malaysian Airlines flight to Kuala Lumpur was delayed for three hours without any word as to why, so when another Malaysian Airlines plane came into land and was going on to Kuala Lumpur we went back through immigration and changed our tickets. Anna was waiting for me there and I didn't want to keep her any longer than I had to.

160 Malaysia

Kuala Lumpur's airport is massive, built in expectation of the city becoming a super hub. It is at least half a kilometre's walk from one end to the other and along the way shopkeepers ran out of their shops enticing us to buy. The Bali bombings have affected the tourist traffic here as well as in Indonesia, and it is clearly difficult for shops to stay operating with so few people passing through.

The airport is 75 kilometres from the city, so by the time we got into town we'd already seen quite a bit of the lush countryside, which was just beginning to open its pores for the beginning of the rainy season. We'd also passed what were once large open-cast tin mines on either side of the road. Tin is a major export of Malaysia and when the mines are exhausted they are filled in and planted with palm-oil trees.

The long-standing president, Mahathir Bin Mohamed, was to resign at the end of the year. One of his legacies would be the fulfilment of his desire to see every family in Malaysia in a decent house. I couldn't believe how much the place had grown since I was last there eight years ago. There were new buildings and apartments everywhere and they were very affordable. A semi-detached apartment in the suburbs cost around $US25,000 and, even though they were cookie-cutters, they were attractive and built in Malaysian materials with a hint of the Orient.

161 Pakistan

The transit stop in Karachi was brief. The flight from Kuala Lumpur, a distance of 4440 kilometres, was much longer than the time we stayed on the ground. I was sorry to see, as we disembarked, a small McDonald's, outside which a long queue was awaiting their dose of Western-style garbage.

We flew to Dubai which we had decided would be our axis for visiting the countries in the Middle East we had been unable to get to before.

CHAPTER EIGHTEEN

Arabia

162 Oman

On 10 January, Peter Fulton, the good mate that he is, drove us past the enormous sand dunes we'd played in at Christmas towards the border between the United Arab Emirates and Oman at a place called Al Wajajah. We turned east and travelled parallel to towering mountains that divide the Emirates from Oman. Sandy dust and morning sunlight combined to create a surreal haze that draped the massif in a soft purple film. As we approached the border, large signs planted in the sand every 50 metres updated us on how far we had to go. But where the sign should have said zero there was only a blown-out concrete building about the size of a ship's container.

On the Oman side, however it was a different story. At a booth in a very substantial building we bought a 28-day visa and decided to drive on until we found some form of habitation in the desert. About eight kilometres down the road, a teetering sign indicated something was down a sandy track. Three kilometres along the track, we topped a small hill to see before us the gleaming white walls of a new village clustered around the disintegrating ruins of an ancient fort.

There was no traffic so our arrival was conspicuous, and three men in boubous as white as the buildings came out to welcome us. They invited us to join them for lunch but we declined, opting instead to see something of the town.

One of the men was the village chairman. His face was craggy with age, his blue eyes rheumy and clouded, but he stood with calm dignity before us. 'I am honoured that you have come to our village,' he said.

We asked him if we could photograph his grandson, against the backdrop of the old stronghold. Khaled Ali Kholfan was a handsome boy of about 12 dressed in a spotless boubou and turban. His flawless youth contrasted with the man-made antiquity of the fort and its one remaining tower, crenellated wall and textured rubble-heaps of pink stone.

We hastened back to Dubai in time for the final of the Kashmir Truck Drivers' Wrestling Match. Peter's family joined us at the edge of the sandy truck-park beside the hotel. We were recognised from the match two weeks before and were ushered to the front of the crowd and offered chairs to sit on next to the prize table. The rest of the crowd, which numbered around 4000, were all men. They stood or squatted in the sand or perched in the dress circle on the cab roofs and trays of a collection of trucks.

One fellow, a Kashmiri restaurant owner in town, leaned across and explained the rules of the tournament to us. They were quite simple. One man held his arm out. His opponent grasped it with two hands and if the contender could break his grip, he was the winner. Each bout lasted between two and three minutes.

To our surprise the master of ceremonies, handsomely attired in a green tunic, officially welcomed us through his loud-hailer. Then he thrust the hailer at me and asked me to respond.

I expressed my desire to visit Kashmir which I believed to be a beautiful country. Applause. I paid tribute to the great skills of the wrestlers and referred to the likelihood of Pakistan's success in the Cricket World Cup. Rousing applause.

'Unfortunately your team will not stand a chance against the might of New Zealanders,' I added. Even more rousing applause.

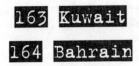

163 Kuwait
164 Bahrain

Next day we transited through Kuwait, where airport security was the most intense we'd experienced. US troops were massing everywhere and the memory of the last Gulf War was still etched in people's minds.

In Bahrain the immigration officer welcomed us: 'It is my very great honour to be the first to stamp your passports in Bahrain,' he said. 'You are very welcome and thank you for coming to visit our land.' With a greeting like that the city had already taken on an attractive dimension.

The choice of airport taxi was limited to a solitary Toyota Camry driven by Mohammed who, although dispossessed of two front teeth, spoke rudimentary English. We asked him to speed us to the Saudi Embassy so we could try for our visas before it closed.

He did his best, but the doors had shut just before we got there. Imagine Mohammed's toothless delight when we asked him to take us instead to the Saudi border. I bet it was the best fare he'd had in a month.

Because Bahrain is an island, its border with Saudi Arabia is in the middle of the King Fahd Causeway, a 25-kilometre long bridge between the two countries.

We drove along the seaside of Manama City, which was now the Arab world's banking centre, past numerous high-rises, prosperous shopping centres and expanses of flat, green parklands. On the foreshore mounted on concrete bases were several old wooden dhows and a high white sculpture of curved beams that held aloft a single pearl. Before oil was discovered here in 1932, pearls from the Persian Gulf were one of the island's main sources of revenue.

165 Saudi Arabia

Getting a visa for Saudi Arabia had been extremely difficult because we'd never found an embassy that was open. We had no option but to see what happened when we reached the causeway.

Despite his poor grasp of the circumstances Mohammed tried to take control at the border by loudly explaining our intention to a group of officers. He sulked extravagantly when one guard came over and talked to us in very good English. We were referred up the ranks and eventually ushered into the office of Rashid Al-Noaimi, the Chief of Police of the causeway border crossing.

We told him that we wanted to step on Saudi soil.

'It is impossible,' he said. 'I have been here for 16 years and it is impossible. You have no visa.' He smiled pleasantly.

'In 16 years,' I said, 'has anyone ever asked if they can do something as crazy as this?'

There was a weighty pause. Rashid said nothing to us but turned and barked an order to a young officer who was passing the door. He was instructed to find a car and drive us to the Saudi side. He then picked up the phone, and spoke to his Saudi counterpart. Whatever he said, it cleared the way.

The young driver was a very excited Ahmed Salah. He'd never crossed the border either. He helped us find the office of the border police Saudi-side, who pretended to be in a meeting rather than come out and meet us. The officer we spoke to refused to sign the book without higher authority. Nonetheless we were on Saudi soil and that was all that mattered. A tall policeman with a scraggy grey beard became curious. We told him what we were doing.

'I cannot sign the book because I am a policeman,' he said. 'But I am also a businessman in the town.'

'Can you sign it as a businessman then,' I said, 'and perhaps you and I can do business one day.'

He grinned and took up the pen.

166 Qatar

We flew to Qatar, a peninsula which juts into the Persian Gulf towards Iran, landing near the capital of Doha. It seemed a dull place. A mere 700,000 people live in Qatar and tourists have been allowed in the country only for the last 12 years. By all accounts there's not much to see.

The next flight from Qatar to Dubai was overbooked but a flight to Abu Dhabi left about the same time. If we could be on it we could then take a taxi to Dubai where we were spending another night. Getting our tickets transferred from Emirates to Qatar Air was, however, no easy task. We were referred to a puffy-faced, paunchy little man with a pencil moustache and an air of importance.

His name was James and we had to launch our own holy war to get him to comply. 'It is *seemingly* simple, *seemingly* simple,' he said. 'But not.'

He took a lot of convincing but after an hour of running all over the airport we won through and flew on to Abu Dhabi on Qatar Air, passing on the way the Quest's 200,000 kilometre mark.

Abu Dhabi's international airport was an extraordinary building, not unlike a series of water tanks on stalks. Inside it looked like a cross between a nightclub and a urinal. Every surface including the ceiling was covered in garishly-coloured tiles.

We jumped in a taxi driven by Jacques from Syria and cruised along the four-lane highway towards Dubai 115 kilometres away. The whole route was lit up like daylight even though we saw only three other cars.

We were back at the Hyatt Apartments by midnight and fell into our beds 20 hours after we'd left them.

CHAPTER NINETEEN

WEST ASIA

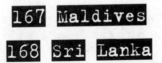

The pilot of the Emirates flight that was to take us through the Maldive Archipelago, southwest of India's southern tip, and on to Colombo was Captain Tim Narara, a stocky Papua New Guinean, with a swaggering cheerfulness and infectious laugh. His crew were Moroccan, Kenyan, Pakistani and English, and they too were infected by his *joie de vivre*.

'If you have been on 200 flights, you must know the inside of a plane,' Tim said when we'd landed at Male Airport. 'Come with me and I'll show you the outside.'

From the tarmac the Airbus 330-200 was a machine of almost ungraspable dimensions – a gargantuan hulk of metal

Sitting in engine with Caption Tim: Maldives.

that despite its size could still manouevre with lumbering delicacy. Feeling like an ant I gazed in awe at the immense starboard engine. 'I've always wanted to sit inside one of those,' I muttered wistfully.

'Why don't you?' said Tim. 'We'll all have a go.' We took turns to jump up and sit on the titanium cowling with the great turbine blades behind us. The three-metre engine casing easily accommodated us all.

Male Airport occupies the whole of one of the 2000 islands and atolls that make up the Maldive Archipelago. The city of Male is on another island and linked to it by a ferry that leaves from the steps of the airport building. As we lifted into a translucent sky I looked down on the myriad islands scattered like white-fringed pebbles across the deep blue sea.

We flew in to Colombo late in the day and, because we were

leaving early the next morning, stayed at the Taj Airport Garden Hotel close by. James left his bag on the plane and it was an hour before he could recover it. Because of the delay we checked in at the hotel at the same time as the Emirates crew, and so we shared dinner with them that night in the hotel restaurant and enjoyed their vivacious company.

169 Brunei

Airline scheduling decreed that we spend another night in Kuala Lumpur in order to get to Brunei. The service on the Royal Brunei flight the following day was, of course, sans alcohol and we arrived at the capital, Bander Seri Begawan, at midnight feeling shattered and yearning for a pick-me-up. Not only was there no beer at the Sheraton Hotel, there was no bar. This tiny, oil-rich, Muslim sultanate on the northwest coast of Borneo completely ignores the existence of alcohol and as a result has a rather subdued nightlife.

We toured the city in a taxi next morning, sliding comfortably through the streets of opulent, structurally fascinating buildings spread between manicured gardens or lush jungle. Omar Ali Saifuddin, the 1958 mosque in the centre of the city, has been exceeded in grandeur by the lavish new mosque, Jame Asr Hassan al Bolkiah, built in 1984, which has four domes covered with real gold and is clad in a geometric pattern of bright blue and white mosaic tiles.

It is a cushy life for the 280,000 people who live in Brunei. Sultan Sir Muda Hassan al Bolkiah Mu'izz-Din-Waddaulah is well known for excesses other than his name, but the citizens also enjoy free education, health and other benefits of the nation's wealth. Our hotel was surprisingly inexpensive. I negotiated a room rate of $US100 at the best hotel in town.

170 Philippines

We were welcomed to the Philippines by a Vodafone network message that informed us that the currency exchange rate was $US1 = PHP53.5. If this innovation had been everywhere, it would have prevented us miscalculating the currencies in many countries. But when we came to catch a taxi it became evident that not everything in Manila was so welcoming. It was late at night and as we walked towards the first taxi on the rank a policeman came bustling over. 'Do not take a taxi. It is too dangerous,' he said. 'Go to where your hotel van is waiting.'

Through a forest of flashing neon signs we were conveyed to our hotel, where a noisy cabaret was in full swing at the bar. Manila was a good-time city, modern, sophisticated and raunchy, and it could leave you exhausted. We quickly swallowed a drink and retreated to the sanctuary of our rooms.

The trip to the airport the next day was on the road that had brought about the resignation of President Corazon Aquino, following allegations that her husband had pocketed half of the millions of pesos intended for its construction. The road lead us to the airport but for Corazon it had been the road to nowhere.

In the context of the Philippines a fraud of such magnitude is made worse by the fact that over 28 million people in the country live below the poverty line, eking out miserable existences in the sort of destitute slums we passed along the infamous road. We stopped at the lights near the airport and wound down the window to give two shabby begging children our remaining pesos. Instantly a babbling group of riffraff tried to climb through the window to grab the money. The driver accelerated off and the beggars both young and old peeled off the car to land in heaps on the road.

At the entrance to the airport was erected a slab of asphalt with the chalked outline of a slain man. This was a monument to

Corazon Aquino's first husband, Benigno Aquino (the chief rival of President Marcos), who was gunned down as he stepped from his plane at Manila Airport on his return from exile in 1983. As we boarded our flight to Taiwan, it was one of the images of Manila I took with me.

171 Taiwan

The Taipei airport was miles from the city, the traffic was dense and noisy and the air polluted. That was all we saw of Taiwan — a boisterous, expensive city wrapped in toxic air where a bewildering confusion of six million people live life in the fastest lane they can find. We stayed the night and rested up for the next day.

172 China

For obvious political reasons there are no direct flights between Taiwan and China. Our only way of getting to Beijing was to fly via Seoul in South Korea. We needed every minute of the time because we were ordered from one end to the other of possibly the longest airport terminal in the world looking for the right transit counter. At the end of a frantic half-hour the right counter turned out to be the one we'd first enquired at.

And there a demure wee ticketing clerk looked at our tickets and said, 'Sorry, fright full.'

'No, no, you don't understand,' I panted. 'We just need a boarding pass.'

She busied herself at her keyboard, paused and, lacking the courage to look me in the eye, said: 'Fright full. Your tickets cancelled.'

James later described my response as maniacal. It certainly

Ulaanbaatar, Mongolia.

felt as if I'd lost my grip. The poor girl hurried off to get support and 10 minutes later another clerk handed us our boarding passes as if she were feeding a crocodile.

'Fright go ereven minutes,' she whispered and pointed down a long corridor.

We boarded to find, once again, that the fright was not at all full.

Beijing's airport is huge and modern with clattery tiled floors and high ceilings. We caught a taxi by ignoring the queue, which was about 200 people long, and flagging a taxi. The driver's English was as non-existent as our Chinese. We tried to get a policeman to tell him where we wanted to go and a very long conversation ensued but none of us were any the wiser. This is one of the biggest barriers to getting around Beijing. English is rarely spoken and the way we pronounce names in Pinyin is not the same as the Chinese do.

The driver nodded a few times and we headed off but after half an hour we could tell we were going around in circles. He had no idea where we were going but was too embarrassed to lose face by telling us. I phoned the hotel. The operator spoke both Mandarin and English and talked him in.

I have always found the Chinese to be amicable and generous and they have a great sense of humour. When we checked in, 'Lucy' and 'Colleen' looked at our small amount of baggage and giggled. 'Too cold,' said Lucy. She went out the back and returned with two traditional Chinese faux-fur hats with drooping spaniel-ear flaps.

Without those hats we'd have been found next day frozen on the pavement of Tiananmen Square or ice-glued to the giant urns in the Forbidden City. There were very few other tourists at these places and no need to wonder why.

173 Mongolia

Mongolia – the very name conjures up images of wild horses and Genghis Khan, of untamed lands and epic journeys by two-humped camels over endless plains of sand. We flew for 1400 kilometres over the vast treeless reaches of the Gobi desert, which was covered in snow and devoid of any sign of vegetable, animal or human life. With only four people per square mile, Mongolia has the lowest population density of any country in the world.

When the plane landed at Buyant-Ukhaa Airport we stepped into a world of icing-sugar snow. We'd thought it cold in Beijing but that was nothing compared to the cold which hit us like an electric shock in the Mongolian capital of Ulaanbaatar. Some eloquent fellow along the way had told us that Mongolia was 'colder than a well-digger's arse'. We now believed him.

We weren't going to be there long, so we ordered a taxi to take us to Sukhbaatar Square, the place from where, in 1921 Damdiny Sukhbaatar had declared Mongolia's independence from China. There had been an ice-carving competition that week and in contrast to the stark Soviet-style buildings around the square rose magnificent white statues, some six metres high, of life-size camels, warriors, kings and horses. They were still frozen solid and sparkled like crushed glass. Laughing groups of children, making the most of the brief appearance of some washed-out sunlight, played around the sculptures and threw themselves with glee down a man-made ice slide.

This compact, quiet city was built along the river Tuul and surrounded by mountains. Most domestic buildings were Soviet-style high-rise apartments but on the fringes of the town were clusters of the traditional felt gers (large dirt-coloured tents). One place of note was the garish Gada Temple, guarded by a larger-than-life Buddha who wore a cloak with a pointed hood.

Not much happens in Ulaanbaataar in winter, but in the warmer summer camels take visitors to desert camps and yak-dung throwing competitions are apparently the centrepiece of the summer festivals.

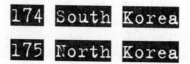

It was astonishing to me that the world's most heavily fortified and militarily-manned border strips, was delineated so close to Seoul. And then their brand-new bells-and-whistles airport was erected almost next door to it.

Incheon Airport is about an hour's congested drive north from downtown Seoul. We could have saved a small fortune and our sanity by catching the bus to the Hyatt Hotel where we were spending the night. Instead we caught a taxi and had to endure the noisy mastication of a gum-chewing driver. It seems that a prerequisite to driving in Seoul is to gnaw on a wad of the stuff as if your life depended on it. One taxi even had a gum-dispensing machine fixed to the driver's arm-rest.

SPC Gang — North Korea.

Getting to North Korea was always going to be a challenge. Recent tensions over the country's possession of nuclear weapons and withdrawal from the Nuclear Non-proliferation Treaty had upped the ante. A year earlier it had looked possible to fly there from Beijing, but that option had gone and the only one left was to join a tour to the Demilitarised Zone (DMZ), which was the first organised tour we had to join on the whole journey. We were accompanied by 30 excited Japanese tourists and another New Zealander, Neil Pakieto and his English bride Louisa. The main commentary was in Japanese but the four of us were assigned to the English-speaking Miss Park.

The DMZ is a four-kilometre-wide strip of land that stretches 241 kilometres across the Korean peninsula. The bus first pulled up at a large building and we filed out to enter the Unification Observatory and Museum from where, but for a heavy mist, we could have seen 17 kilometres into North Korea. Below the building were a stack of speakers which boomed South Korean propaganda messages and military music towards North Korea.

And then through the fog messages started booming back

from North Korea. It was very bizarre. As was the fact that we were still in South Korea but on the walls of the museum were many images of Kim Jong-il, the communist leader of North Korea since 1997. Miss Park, a tiny, prim Korean woman whose head was warmly cocooned in a large tea-cosy hat, whispered to us that his passions were the three Ws – weapons, women and wine.

Miss Park was her own propaganda machine.

'When the South Koreans erected a 100-metre flagpole,' she said, 'the North Koreans built theirs 160 metres high, but they have to take the flag down every night, so that it doesn't wear out. They can't afford a new one.'

She pointed out the two villages in the DMZ and hissed: 'In the South Korean Tai Song Dong "Freedom Village" people have a very good life. In the North Korean Gi Jong Dong "Propaganda Village" they have a dreadful time.'

We were ushered back onto the bus and driven to Camp Bonifas where many of the 35,000 US soldiers in Korea are based. There we had lunch, queuing in the mess hall for our dollops of spuds, chipolatas, chicken drumsticks, mixed vegetables and mountainous piles of bread rolls. It was like a scene from *M*A*S*H*.

We were then marshalled into the lecture hall for a potted history lesson, and handed declaration papers to sign. Basically they stated that if we got shot it was our own problem and we agreed that we would not undertake any gesture, smile, wave or expression that could be misconstrued by the North Korean side. A one-finger salute would possibly start World War III. We were, however, permitted if not encouraged to take photographs.

For the final push to the front, we were shepherded onto a bus. Fully-armed servicemen, SPC (specialist) Gang, stood ramrod-straight facing us at the front to escort us into the Joint Service Area, a small neutral area in the centre of the DMZ.

We alighted at the Panmunjom Command Centre and SPC Gang issued commands as sharp as a knife, sending Miss Park into a nervous spasm. James and I had not come to heel. 'Pleeeeease,' she begged, 'you *must* stand in line.'

In crocodile formation we were marched to a pagoda-shaped observation building overlooking three blue Military Armistice Commission huts and behind them the North Korean command building. Five hundred soldiers from South Korea and the USA are based in the Joint Service Area. The South Korean soldiers, standing guard over the huts, exposed only the left or right sides of their bodies from behind the walls. By way of contrast, at the entrance of their command building the North Koreans stood fully exposed, watching through binoculars.

We were then marched down and allowed to enter the middle hut, the very one where the Armistice was signed in 1953, exactly 50 years ago. Inside we walked to the North Korean side and had photographs taken on North Korean floorboards. North Korea was ticked off the list.

Miss Park relaxed once we were back on the bus, relieved no doubt that we had not started World War III. We transferred back to our original bus and headed back to Seoul.

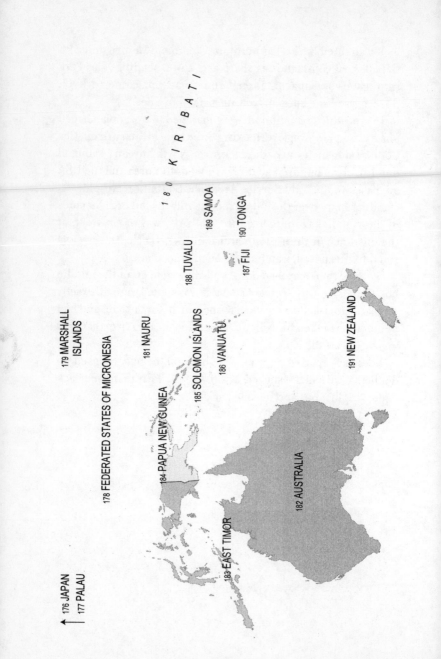

176 JAPAN
177 PALAU

179 MARSHALL
ISLANDS

178 FEDERATED STATES OF MICRONESIA

181 NAURU

185 SOLOMON ISLANDS

184 PAPUA NEW GUINEA

186 VANUATU

183 EAST TIMOR

182 AUSTRALIA

188 TUVALU

189 SAMOA

190 TONGA

187 FIJI

K I R I B A T I

1 8 0

191 NEW ZEALAND

CHAPTER TWENTY

THE PACIFIC

176 Japan

The choice was simple: mortgage the house so we could overnight near Narita Airport in a room the size of a cupboard, or head out on the next flight to Guam. We chose the latter. The airport is as large as a small nation and one of the most efficient in the world. We were met at the entrance by two charming young Japanese women in bright red uniforms who ushered us onto a bus to the next terminal. We had onward boarding passes within minutes, marched through immigration past officers wearing protective face-masks, and then at the top of the airbridge were searched by a security officer who gave a deep bow and said, 'Sorry for delay.' As far as we were concerned there hadn't been any.

Although Guam is a territory of the United States and

therefore not in the 'nation' category, we still had to pass through it to get to Micronesia. We arrived at night and only the next morning saw the remains of the damage that a typhoon had wrought as it ripped through there only a month and a half ago.

Twelve hours of officially recorded 180-mph winds (which were in reality much higher) had savaged the beachfront, stripping coconut palms of their fronds so that they looked like a forest of bent billiard cues. The wind gauge at Anderson Airforce base – guaranteed accurate up to 180 mph – had been ripped off the roof it was bolted to. Cars were lifted into the air and deposited elsewhere, the fuel dump had burst into flames and hundreds of homes had disappeared skyward.

We were staying at the Hyatt Hotel which was undamaged, apart from a few windows which had been sucked from their sockets at the rear of the hotel. Although this tiny island was tropical it didn't project an image of paradise: it was best known for its duty-free shopping and for boasting the world's largest K-Mart. The dominant religion is Roman Catholic and the one thing we would have liked to have seen in Hagatra City was the pirouetting pontiff, a twirling statue of Pope John II erected on the site where he held mass in 1981.

The security screening at Antonio B Won Pat Guam International Air Terminal for the flight to Palau was excessively sensitive. Even the metal eyelets in our shoes set off the scanner alarms. I took off my shoes, then my belt, watched by a middle-aged, black woman officer who eyed me sternly.

I eyed her back. 'This is as far as I go on the first date,' I said.

Her face collapsed with amusement: 'That's what all the guys say,' she retorted. 'Hey but look at me! How could you resist?' She waggled her generous hips provocatively.

177 Palau

At the airport tourist office on the island of Koror, we met Blanche who recommended we stay at the Penthouse Hotel, which we later learned was owned by her family. She told us she was a judge for the island's Mr and Miss Competition that was being held in the school hall that night, and invited us to attend.

The large hall was festooned with palm fronds and other tropical foliage, but fashion in this far-flung American outpost was straight from the States. The boys wore basketball uniforms and the leggy girls with skins like polished copper paraded in skimpy bikinis and carried beachballs. The heat in the hall was so intense that we wilted and left long before the final judgement.

Although men were elected to government in Micronesia, the line of descent passed down through the women, who therefore owned much of the land. There was a wise rationale for this: you always knew who your mother was but not necessarily your father.

The society was matriarchal in other aspects. One recent story was about a DJ at the local radio station who aired a few maverick views. These upset the local branch of the women's group who told him to take them back or they would make his mother responsible. He refused. The women made good their threat and the mother was fined $US2000 for not exercising enough control over her son. The DJ made a public apology, and was not heard again.

The seat of government, currently on Palau, was being shifted to the neighbouring island of Babeldoab and into a new, sparkling white parliament building which emulated Washington's Capitol building.

178 Federated States of Micronesia

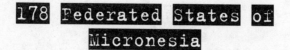

We flew over a milky blue Pacific Ocean and the myriad jungle-covered islands, dotted with huts and rearing granite columns, which make up the archipelago of the Federated States of Micronesia (formerly the Caroline Islands). Along the way we landed and spent an hour at each of the airports of Truk (also known and pronounced as Chuuk), Pohnpei and Kosrae Islands, which make up three of the four states.

Micronesia was ruled by Spain, Germany, Japan and then, after World War II until independence in 1991, it was administered by the US which still retains responsibility for its defence. During the war Truk was one of Japan's most important bases in the Pacific Ocean. Tourists now go there to scuba dive among the numerous wartime wrecks drowned in the lagoon formed by the coral reef that rings the islands and their sandy shoreline.

179 Marshall Islands

The second-to-last stop on this Micronesian milk-run flight was at Kwajalein. This is the Marshall Islands' largest coral atoll, which is why the 1100-square-mile lagoon is deemed perfect for catching intercontinental ballistic missiles launched from Vandenberg Air Force Base in California. The ICBMs take only 28 minutes to travel the 4760 kilometres: most land in the lagoon.

Between missiles, the 2700 American-civilian contractors and their families based on the atoll play golf on the nine-hole course, go cycling or mow the capacious lawns that separate the military buildings, satellite dishes and large rounded tracking domes.

Left, Senator Ismael John from Eniwetak, and right,
Imata Kabua, paramount chief, Kwajalein.

I'd bought the day's edition of the *Guam Pacific Daily News*.
Waiting on board, I read how the Marshall Islands' government
had signed a new 83-year lease to retain the US airforce base.
This had decidedly miffed the Kwajalein people because they
had not been informed, and there was still 13 years to run on the
existing lease. The article was illustrated by a picture of the
atoll's Irorj Laplap (paramount chief), the former president of
the Marshall Islands, Imata Kabua. I lowered the paper and there
sitting next to me was the man himself.

It was a coincidence worth exploring. 'Imata Kabua, I
presume?' I ventured. He smiled, a wreath of goodwill. Imata
Kabua only came up to my shoulders in height but he conducted
himself with an air of authority; and although his coppery skin
was creased by age and his hair was steely grey, his enthusiasm
for his homeland had not diminished.

As senator of Kwajalein he was off to the nation's capital,
Dalap-Uliga-Darrit on Majuro atoll, to propose a vote of no
confidence in the government for this underhand dealing.

As we flew on towards Majuro, Imata told me how in 1982 he'd
led an occupation of the Boy Scout camp situated bang in the
middle of the US base, to protest about the base being planted on

the island without any compensation for his people. The sit-in lasted from July to October and as a result he had been flown to Washington to sign a lease that had earned the island $US11 million a year ever since.

On Majuro there were only two hotels. We decided on the Robert Reimers for the simple reason that the name intrigued us. As it turned out it was the place to be. It was the centre for everything that happened on the atoll and, although the décor was a little tired, the fish in the restaurant that night was so fresh it was almost flapping.

Several of the Marshall Islands senators who were joining Imata's new protest were in the breakfast room next morning. Imata introduced us to Senator Ismael John from Eniwetak and Bikini atolls. Atop his bulging frame, his crumpled moon-face was cast in an expression of sadness. He had good reason to feel forlorn. The Americans have never properly compensated the inhabitants of Bikini atoll for dispossessing them of their home, using it as a test site for nuclear bombs and the resulting con-tamination. The first peace-time nuclear bomb was detonated on Bikini atoll in 1947, followed by a further 44 over the next 11 years.

180 Kiribati

We flew south on a Dornier 228, passing over a string of atolls, each no bigger than a cricket pitch and encircled by glistening white beaches. These were some of the 33 atolls that make up the Republic of Kiribati (pronounced Kiribass) and straddle both the International Date Line and the equator. Before we landed on the island of Tarawa, the pilot buzzed the strip to clear it of animals, islanders and drying washing.

Some weeks before, we'd made a reservation at the island's only hotel, which was government-run. The Otintei, a plain concrete-block building suffocated by palm trees, pushed the Guest House Zanderij in Suriname into second place. There was no record of our reservation, I had to pay 15 percent surcharge just to use my credit card, the rooms were dingy, the carpets threadbare and the bed linen smelled thickly of chlorine. To cap it off, in the restaurant that night all but three tables had been moved upstairs for a function for the Australian High Commission; so, it appeared, had most of the food and all but one waitress.

Tarawa was the scene of the bloodiest battle of the Pacific in World War II. While in Majuro, we'd met Utz Welner, who had spent most of his working life in the Pacific and had become deeply interested in its war history. He'd asked us if we would take a photograph of Red Beach Two for him because it was one of the few battle sites he hadn't seen. We had been recommended to locate a man called John Brown who runs the historical tour on the island, but he was too busy to help.

But we had read that near the village of Betio there was a tourist office and we set off to find it − a difficult assignment because no one we asked had heard of it, including the duty policemen at the police station next door. Then when we did locate it, the three fresh-faced staff looked at me blankly when I mentioned Red Beach Two.

'It was only the site of one of the bloodiest battles of the Pacific war,' I barked, and began to educate them about their own history − how the Americans had invaded the island at low tide and become stuck within easy firing range of Japanese guns, which had wiped them out almost to a man.

We ferreted around their office, found a map and Red Beach turned out to be just down the road the other side of an immense rubbish dump which was bisected by a rudimentary track. Wobbling along on a rusty bicycle came a bushy-haired, pot-bellied old man in shorts and a tattered Calvin Klein singlet. He spoke excellent English.

'I was a merchant seaman and went all over the world,' he grinned, displaying a mouth almost devoid of teeth. 'I know everything about Red Beach Two. My father took me to Nauru Island to get me away from the Japanese but I remember the stories well.'

We paid him an unsolicited five dollars to be our guide and, although the tide was in, he pointed out the turret of a Sherman tank jutting out of the water, set against the backdrop of the remnants of around 20 boats which had been grounded by the locals. On land about 30 metres back from the retaining wall, a concrete Japanese bunker now sprouted moss and weeds.

In a minivan which had been altered to hold 10 more passengers than the intended 12, we bounced along the one road on the island accompanied by blaring music to visit the Australian Embassy and have the record book witnessed. Third Secretary Tim Davies obliged. This young red-headed Australian said he was thrilled that he still had two years of his three-year post left. He loved island life – the climate, the music, the food and the people.

'What about all those discarded VB Bitter cans and other rubbish?' I said. 'How can you be happy here with those just about drowning the atoll?'

'Ah, you noticed,' he said, as if there was two, not 200,000. 'Kiribati is the second-largest consumer of VB Bitter after Australia. And re-exporting the empties to Australia for recycling is the second-biggest export earner for the nation, bringing in $40,000 of revenue a year.' Number one is obviously foreign aid.

Tim was also at the airport next day, sweating so profusely in the humid heat that he looked as if he'd fallen in the lagoon. He was still protesting his love of the place, a sentiment we found difficult to share.

James and I stood talking to Tim in the hammering sun outside until a young woman came and asked for our passports.

Five minutes later she returned with them stamped, and suggested that some time soon it would be a good idea to board the plane. We had no argument with that.

181 Nauru

In Nauru we stopped long enough to get another passport stamp and were looked after by Ernest Stephen, chief of operations, who strolled up to us in his flowery Hawaiian shirt and oversaw our two-minute arrival and departure.

From the air I looked down on this 20 square kilometres of bird guano and what appeared to be a heavy carpet of foliage covering the island. This belied the fact that much of the island is a worked-out quarry where only 80 percent of the land is now inhabitable. Phosphate mining brought a prosperity to the island that is almost unknown in this part of the world. The 7000 inhabitants had lived the life of Riley with imported luxuries and flash cars. Some of the profit had been invested in a trust fund to fill the gap when the phosphate ran out (predicted to be in 2006), but because of bad management its returns will not save Nauru from economic collapse. On a slope and barely visible through the trees we saw the camp that harbours the asylum seekers from the *Tampa* and *Tobruk* who, in an Australian operation called the 'Pacific Solution', had been transported here in 2001.

This refugee camp, paid for by the Australians, was largely why we didn't stay on Nauru. Visas were virtually impossible to get now following some foreign journalists posing as tourists and filing negative articles on the camp.

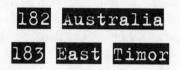

182 Australia
183 East Timor

Our arrival in Brisbane came with mixed feelings. James was so keen to get home he beat me through the immigration gate, which was very unusual. I stayed the night at a hotel in town. For the first time in months we were on familiar soil and the end of the Quest was in sight. We had two weeks of travel left but our enthusiasm was definitely waning. When we met at the airport next morning we were both glum and apathetic about moving on.

East Timor was not easy to get to. It seemed that our only choice was to catch a flight from Darwin: we decided to return on the same aircraft that afternoon. It was probably tiredness and the proximity of home that caused us to make one of the worst decisions of the trip, which was not to spend the night in Dili but to return to a much-less-interesting Darwin.

There were UN personnel still hanging about the Dili Airport but apart from them, no sign at all of the bloodshed and turmoil that had recently brought East Timor its independence.

As we took off to the northwest, turned and flew past the city bathed in the last light of day, everything looked as calm and peaceful as a Sunday morning.

184 Papua New Guinea

We'd felt some trepidation about going to Port Moresby because we'd been warned over and over to be very careful, without a full explanation as to why. I worried for the two witless Australian girls who were wandering around the plane dressed in seriously skimpy clothing, probably imagining they were off to some-where like the Bahamas.

The queues at immigration hinted at what was happening in the country. There were three counters: one for PNG nationals (five off our flight); another for the 15 residents; and behind the third stood the rest of the planeload of passengers, forming a snaking line around a corner and back up the stairs. This queue was mostly made up of men carrying briefcases and laptops whom we guessed to be there on business.

Outside the terminal was an unruly wall of New Guinean men. I watched the witless girls take one look and flee back inside.

We climbed into the hotel courtesy van. Travelling with us to Port Moresby was Gerald, an Australian who had been coming to PNG on business for nearly 30 years. He backed up what we'd deduced from the queues.

'Everyone makes a buck out of PNG except its inhabitants,' he said. 'The place is stuffed with minerals and oil but anything over six feet below ground level belongs to the state. The government issues licences to foreign companies ensuring that 22 percent of the declared revenue supposedly returns to the state and a pathetic two percent goes to the landowners. And yet, no matter how much the island is pillaged, the declared revenue doesn't seem to vary.'

According to Gerald, most of the government's share never got as far as the coffers, let alone the people: 'This does nothing to relieve the 60 percent unemployment and rising crime rates, as disadvantaged citizens take up the professions of extortion and violent assault in a last-ditch effort to support themselves.'

The streets of Port Moresby were calm as we were whisked through to the Crown Plaza Hotel high on a hill overlooking some of the town's best real estate and the sapphire water of the bay. The route we took had been carefully planned to shield us from the sights of poverty. The hotel was heavily guarded by a barbed wire-topped wall and a formidable steel gate, but inside was all landscaped garden and finely furnished interiors.

At the airport next day, taking pride of place in the departure lounge was a large picture of a once-lofty jungle-covered mountain that had been decapitated by mining. It rather summed things up.

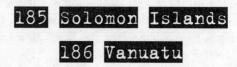

185 Solomon Islands
186 Vanuatu

We flew back to Brisbane for another two days and on the morning of 10 February flew out on Solomon Islands Air for the last section of the Quest. First was a quick touch-down in Henderson International Airport at Honiara in the Solomon Islands and then on to Port Vila in Vanuatu.

We transited through Port Vila on the island of Efate, the capital of these glittering green islands which are surrounded by a sea as blue as a child's first painting. But not all has been well in this geographical paradise. It was the source of blackbirding (South Seas slavery) in the late 19th century, and many Vanuatuans ended up in the sugar-cane fields of Fiji and northern Australia, never to return to their homeland. More recently, in 1996, there were allegations of massive fraud by members of the Carlot Korman government. As our Australian mate Utz had put it: 'They [the fraudsters] invested in a sure thing – a sure thing no one would ever see the money again.'

187 Fiji

This, of course, was familiar territory. The Nadi Sheraton wouldn't lower their expensive room rates so we went to the more affordable Mocambo Hotel with its thatched roof and traditional décor.

The next country we were going to was Tuvalu but only one flight leaves each week from Suva. We had two days up our sleeves and long-time Suva friends Stuart and Gilly Huggart offered to have us to stay. Home comforts were like a holiday but now that we were close to our own home, there was an increasing number of media enquiries to attend to.

At the Huggarts' dinner table, talk turned to global affairs and for the first time I realised that despite our cursory visits to some countries I had gained a considerable overview of the cause and effect of events around the globe. I could at least haul out a mental image of the places we talked about and, more often than not, a photograph or two.

188 Tuvalu

The flight was delayed for hours while a problem with the landing system at Tuvalu airport was being solved. There was no sustenance at the airport and the smoking lounge was back on the other side of immigration and no, I couldn't pop out for a smoke.

After two hours I was getting desperate, and then a security officer, more sympathetic than others, relented and allowed me to re-enter the country to further wreck my lungs Fiji-side. I had to leave him my passport.

It was a fortuitous puff because at the Pacific Link check-in desk I happened to hear that James and I were being off-loaded. In case the flight could not land in Tuvalu, weight was being shed to enable the plane to return. I was able to persuade them to reinstate us.

An hour later we headed north, feeling guilty about the two bulky fellows we'd displaced who would now not see their families again for a week.

Tuvalu is a group of tiny islands and atolls of eroded coral in the western Pacific Ocean. We'd heard that Funafuti, like Kiribati, was just another rubbish dump, but what we saw around

the airport seemed perfectly well maintained. The extraordinary
thing about Tuvalu is that the total area of dry land is a mere 16
square kilometres but the islands form a chain 570 kilometres
long. Their highest point is 4.6 metres above sea level, and if
global warming accelerates and sea levels rise, the islands are in
grave danger of drowning.

189 Samoa

It was 11 February, the penultimate day of the Quest. At Nadi
Airport a Fijian television crew filmed us for the *Holmes* show in
New Zealand, and everybody waiting around found this staged
affair a great way to fill in time. We, on the other hand, found
little to amuse us during our eight-hour wait for the flight to
Samoa and home.

It was after midnight when we got to Apia. To our surprise,
Jennifer McDonald, a youthful blonde who was New Zealand's
deputy high commissioner, was there to meet us. She kept us

Deputy High Commissioner, Samoa.

company for four hours. Such generosity was typical of the way we had been welcomed and looked after by New Zealanders in many parts of the world. I determined that I would in future, always do the same.

190 Tonga
191 New Zealand

If ever we'd thought that Air New Zealand might have made a bit of a fuss of our final two flights of the Quest, we were wrong. Completely unsung, we touched down at Tonga's Fua'amotu International Airport and entered and exited the country within 10 minutes. Then we stood in the lacklustre departure lounge and watched a group of young American tourists conducting video interviews on each other. 'Are you having a good time?' they asked. 'Do you like all this flying?'

At that stage I wasn't sure whether I would say yes or no if they asked me the same questions. We were just about to end 240,000 kilometres aloft on 104 airlines in 54 different types of plane. Both of us were feeling deflated and dead-tired, but from that point our thoughts differed. I wanted to keep going. I suggested to James that we 'knock off' all the territories in the world as well. He was pining for home and he looked at me in stunned horror: 'Have you completely lost your diminutive pile of marbles?' he groaned.

We exchanged exhausted glances.

'I never had any,' I grinned. 'I always told you the whole idea was crazy.'

EPILOGUE

Opportunities multiply as they are seized.

Sun Tzu

This was never more obvious than when we set out to photograph children for *My Dream*, the other book to be published from the Quest. It was planned from the outset to support the Save the Children Fund, in ways not only financial. Conceived in a rash, time-rich moment prior to our departure, photographing and recording the dream of one child in every country we visited quickly became the reason for the journey.

Taking photographs for *My Dream*, in spite of often being dog-tired and exasperated, became the reason we explored every place we visited, however briefly. And the feeling of elation we experienced once the photograph and the dream were safely recorded, buoyed us sufficiently to get through the rest of that day and the next. We found children the world over were always honest and pragmatic, even amidst the most deprived of circumstances.

We decided the children were to be found by chance, so this often led us to locations no tourist would ever venture into, for obvious reasons. It was our experiences in these places that will remain with us forever: an arid village on the Somaliland border with Djibouti; the village on the outskirts of Nairobi, Kenya, where essential services amounted to a tap on the main street; sitting in a deserted café beside Lake Ohrid, Macedonia, on a cold winter's day, listening to the story unfold of a six-year-old boy losing his parents when he was one and now about to lose his only remaining family, his grandmother, to old age. Despite the futility of it all, he was begging for money to buy medicine for her.

The dreams, which were recorded unprompted and verbatim, gave us a brief yet salutary understanding of the nations we were visiting, as well as a feeling of complete and utter hopelessness as individuals to bring about any meaningful change to what is largely a wretched world. We were constantly reminded about what an essential job groups like Save the Children are doing across the globe.

The passion to travel, to explore the unknown, to put oneself into unfamiliar, exciting and scary situations all inspired the Quest in the first place. This was our motivation to continue when things, as they often did, became unbearably tough. There were only a few who understood the innate madness of the Quest. They ranged from, ironically, the immigration officers in some of the most impoverished countries on the planet, to kindly expat New Zealanders in far-flung lands, who were in turn pursuing their dreams.

Would I do it again . . . absolutely.

Would I do it the same way . . . no.

Yes, we visited 191 countries and, yes, we gained a fleeting impression of them all, an understanding that only our transitional and gradual leaping from country to adjoining country could afford. But next time – if I'm lucky enough to get a next time – I would do it more slowly, spending time in countries the world knows little about, or as we came to realise, has conveniently forgotten.

James

The days that have stuck in my mind are those that were quite unplanned or when we had to change at the last minute just to keep going. From West Africa onwards, the idea of making progress became psychologically important even when we knew we needed time off to catch up on sleep/washing/change arrangements/file reports and so on.

Much of the journey is a blur. A comment can take me back to a particular event or country, but I know that only about 20 percent of the Quest will remain in my memory.

I suffered from homesickness in the first three weeks. I really appreciated John's offer to fly Nicola to join me in New York. The pace quickened after that and I was able to put 'home and family' in a box and file it to one side for longer periods.

Certain days I could never forget. Crossing into Somalia from Djibouti: on a Muslim holy day when the border was technically closed; sitting chewing qat with the border police with the Red Sea as a backdrop; flying over snow-covered mountains into Ulaanbaataar in Mongolia and photographing children in the square in a temperature of minus 11 degrees Centigrade; walking around Tiananmen Square and the Forbidden City in Beijing.

I saw the encouraging signs of good ecological practices in some parts of the world, although there are many more problems to be overcome. I remember sitting with a white Zimbabwean businessman and his Gabonese colleague in Libreville who said that you can see hippos and crocs body-surfing on some beaches in Gabon, and that fishermen along the river systems of the country claim that gorillas are so unafraid that they will approach humans.

Those we met were all decent human beings and I couldn't get over people's brave humour even when their circumstances were no laughing matter. I was bowled over by the hospitality shown us in parts of Africa and the Middle East, which I hadn't expected.

The Quest has taught me other things. I am considerably more relaxed than I was before I left. I've learned to put up with situations that I would once have rebelled against and to be more diplomatic. I learned to operate out of my comfort zone and take on board one of John's philosophies, which was: 'Don't piss your pants until it happens.' That helped me sleep at night on more than one occasion.

From a travel agent's perspective I was discouraged to find that the best-laid plans using the best theory did not actually work in reality, which has made me rethink how I will do things in the future.

I will now dig deeper to make donations to certain aid organisations – those I can be certain do *not* give cash or valuable resources to tyrannical and/or corrupt regimes. I think the key to breaking the cycle of poverty is to empower local people to help themselves, and this requires education. Sadly, the only visible sign of success in some of the foreign aid operations we saw was by Toyota, which seems to have supplied most of the aid groups with Landcruisers.

One rewarding but sometimes saddening thing we did was going out, when we often would rather have slept, to find children to photograph. The conditions in which children are often forced to live are appalling. Children are our future and by messing up generations of them by war, abuse, famine and neglect, the well-being of the world can never develop.

Another lesson I learned was to be flexible, think laterally and, if an opportunity arises, take it now. It might not be there when you return later.

www.allnationsquest.com
www.mydream.co.nz